How Serious a Threat a Threat Are Online Predators?

Patricia D. Netzley

INCONTROVERSY

ReferencePoint
Press®

San Diego, CA

For more information, contact:
ReferencePoint Press, Inc.
PO Box 27779
San Diego, CA 92198
www.ReferencePointPress.com

LIBRARY OF CONGRESS CATALOGING-IN-PUBLICATION DATA

Netzley, Patricia D.
    How serious a threat are online predators? / by Patricia D. Netzley.
        p. cm. -- (Controversy series)
    Includes bibliographical references and index.
    ISBN 978-1-60152-450-8 (hardback) -- ISBN 1-60152-450-1 (hardback)
 1. Online sexual predators--Juvenile literature. 2. Internet--Safety measures--Juvenile literature. 3. Internet and teenagers--Juvenile literature. 4. Internet and children--Juvenile literature. I. Title.
    HV6773.15.O58N48   2013
    364.15'3—dc23
                                                                                              2012005901

Contents

Foreword   4

Introduction
Online Victimization   6

Chapter One
What Are the Origins of the Online Predator Problem?   12

Chapter Two
Who Is Most at Risk from Online Predators?   26

Chapter Three
Are Internet Dangers Exaggerated?   39

Chapter Four
Can the Legal System Stop Online Predators?   52

Chapter Five
Can Prevention Efforts Protect Online Users from
Predators?   64

Related Organizations and Websites   78

Additional Reading   83

Source Notes   85

Index   91

Picture Credits   95

About the Author   96

Foreword

In 2008, as the US economy and economies worldwide were falling into the worst recession since the Great Depression, most Americans had difficulty comprehending the complexity, magnitude, and scope of what was happening. As is often the case with a complex, controversial issue such as this historic global economic recession, looking at the problem as a whole can be overwhelming and often does not lead to understanding. One way to better comprehend such a large issue or event is to break it into smaller parts. The intricacies of global economic recession may be difficult to understand, but one can gain insight by instead beginning with an individual contributing factor, such as the real estate market. When examined through a narrower lens, complex issues become clearer and easier to evaluate.

This is the idea behind ReferencePoint Press's *In Controversy* series. The series examines the complex, controversial issues of the day by breaking them into smaller pieces. Rather than looking at the stem cell research debate as a whole, a title would examine an important aspect of the debate such as *Is Stem Cell Research Necessary?* or *Is Embryonic Stem Cell Research Ethical?* By studying the central issues of the debate individually, researchers gain a more solid and focused understanding of the topic as a whole.

Each book in the series provides a clear, insightful discussion of the issues, integrating facts and a variety of contrasting opinions for a solid, balanced perspective. Personal accounts and direct quotes from academic and professional experts, advocacy groups, politicians, and others enhance the narrative. Sidebars add depth to the discussion by expanding on important ideas and events. For quick reference, a list of key facts concludes every chapter. Source notes, an annotated organizations list, bibliography, and index provide student researchers with additional tools for papers and class discussion.

The *In Controversy* series also challenges students to think critically about issues, to improve their problem-solving skills, and to sharpen their ability to form educated opinions. As President Barack Obama stated in a March 2009 speech, success in the twenty-first century will not be measurable merely by students' ability to "fill in a bubble on a test but whether they possess 21st century skills like problem-solving and critical thinking and entrepreneurship and creativity." Those who possess these skills will have a strong foundation for whatever lies ahead.

No one can know for certain what sort of world awaits today's students. What we can assume, however, is that those who are inquisitive about a wide range of issues; open-minded to divergent views; aware of bias and opinion; and able to reason, reflect, and reconsider will be best prepared for the future. As the international development organization Oxfam notes, "Today's young people will grow up to be the citizens of the future: but what that future holds for them is uncertain. We can be quite confident, however, that they will be faced with decisions about a wide range of issues on which people have differing, contradictory views. If they are to develop as global citizens all young people should have the opportunity to engage with these controversial issues."

In Controversy helps today's students better prepare for tomorrow. An understanding of the complex issues that drive our world and the ability to think critically about them are essential components of contributing, competing, and succeeding in the twenty-first century.

Online Victimization

I n September 2011 a 15-year-old girl from Buena Park, California, traveled over 100 miles by bus to Cathedral City, California, in order to meet someone she had befriended on the social website Facebook two years earlier. The teen believed that her Facebook friend, who paid for her bus ticket, was visiting California from Italy and that he was a 17-year-old boy named Giovanni Antonio Corsentino. She planned to travel with him from Cathedral City to Arizona, where her brother lived.

But when she arrived at the house where "Giovanni" was supposedly staying, the girl discovered that he was actually 44-year-old Jeffrey Thomas Sackman. Sackman imprisoned her in his home, drugged her with methamphetamines, and raped her over a period of several days. Meanwhile, her mother used cell phone records to figure out where she had gone and sent police to rescue her.

Many Victims

After Sackman was arrested, investigators discovered that the Buena Park teen was not his only victim. He had done the same thing to at least three other girls and had been posing as a boy online, using various names, for at least six years. When news of his actions spread through Cathedral City, students at the town's college expressed disbelief that anyone would develop a friendship with a Facebook stranger. "I only add people [as friends on Facebook] that I know," said one teen, Ashley. But this same girl then admitted that she did make friends with strangers on another social networking website, MySpace, and added, "I've made mistakes in the past, so have a lot of people, but now I only talk to people that I know."[1]

In researching the use of MySpace, which has roughly 40 million users, Pete Williams of NBC News found that many users share enough information to allow a stranger to figure out where they live, work, or go to school. Some users even provide their phone numbers and/or home addresses. "You can create relationships on MySpace," one of these users, a high school sophomore, told Williams. "Or you can create friendships."[2] But Williams counters this notion by citing cases in which a man used information gleaned from MySpace or Facebook in order to track down girls and rape them.

Because such stories attract media attention, many people know that sharing too much information with strangers online is unwise. Nonetheless, recent studies have found that approximately one-fourth of teenagers chat regularly with strangers at social networking sites. Research also suggests that four out of five young people have trouble determining the age of the person with whom they are communicating. Online, teens can come across as adults and vice versa, especially those who are intentionally trying to deceive people in a chat room. Gender can be difficult to determine as well, as evidenced by the fact that one of the most successful online financial frauds involves a man pretending to be a woman in order to get the victim to send "her" money.

False Identities

According to DatingSitesReviews.com, an estimated 10 percent of the new accounts created on free dating websites each day are false identities made to deceive others. Reliable statistics regarding just how many people fall for such deceptions do not exist, however, because victims are often too embarrassed to come forward. Still, the situation is known to be serious enough for the US Department of State to caution Americans about the risk of putting too much trust in the "friends" they make online. The department's website warns, "The anonymity of the Internet means that the U.S. citizen cannot be sure of the real name, age, marital status, nationality, or even gender of the correspondent."[3]

This anonymity has been a boon to predators—individuals who victimize others, typically for personal satisfaction and/or monetary gain. Predators can achieve these things without alert-

The anonymity of communication in the digital age presents many new opportunities for online predators. They can gain private information or make personal connections by pretending to be something—or someone—they are not.

ing the victim to their presence. For example, they can use the Internet to steal stored computer data that will allow them to raid someone's bank account and/or destroy that person's credit without the victim knowing about the theft until long afterward. But some predators prefer to con the victim into interacting in ways that bring the predator personal and/or financial satisfaction. This is the kind of victimization that most people think of when they hear the term "online predator."

The Internet provides such criminals with far more potential victims than they could reach otherwise. In 2011 there were 2 billion Internet subscribers worldwide, and Facebook had approximately 800 million active users. In addition, 90 percent of teens and young adults and 75 percent of adults in the United States reported going online several times a week, and more than 60 percent of adults over age 55 said they went online significantly more often in 2011 than the previous year.

The Scope of the Problem

A similar rise has occurred in the number of people who go online specifically to prey on others. In fact, so many predators are exploiting the anonymity of the Internet that law enforcement agencies are often overwhelmed by the challenge of combating them. For example, in 2009 officials with a Wisconsin task force charged with fighting sexual predation complained publicly about the need for more resources to deal with the problem. One of the task force's agents, Jennifer Price, says, "We've got so many offenders out there. I just see the balloon getting bigger and bigger and bigger."[4] This is true in regard to financial predation as well, as evidenced by the fact that in November 2010 the Internet Fraud Complaint Center (IFCC)—just one of many places where a victim of a financial predator can report a crime—received its 2 millionth complaint.

However, the University of New Hampshire Crimes Against Children Research Center suggests that online predation is not a growing problem, just an ongoing problem. In discussing sexual predation that targets teens, researchers with the Center say that "the facts do not suggest that the Internet is facilitating an epidemic of sex crimes against youth. Rather, increasing arrests for online predation probably reflect increasing rates of youth internet use, a migration of crime from offline to online venues, and the growth of law enforcement activity against online crimes."[5] In other words, there only seem to be more predators because there are more Internet users and more opportunities for predation, and because law enforcement agencies have only recently begun to deal with the problem of online predation.

> "The danger to children, whether they are from New York or New Zealand, has drastically increased."[8]
>
> — Donna Rice Hughes, founder of Enough is Enough, an Internet safety organization.

Risk Assessment

But while online predation might not be an epidemic, the common perception is that Internet users are at great risk for being victimized online. Studies show that two-thirds of mothers, for example, believe that the Internet is just as or more dangerous for their teenagers than drunk driving. But Internet safety expert

Larry Magid says, "That might be how moms feel, but it's not reflective of the real world. While moms have good reason to be concerned about how their teens use the Internet, online dangers pale compared to the risks of drunk driving."[6]

Magid is correct in his risk assessment. According to the organization Mothers Against Drunk Driving (MADD), "Car crashes are the leading cause of death for teens, and one out of three of those is alcohol related."[7] But many people counter that regardless of how dangerous the Internet is when compared to other activities, it is still a dangerous place, and the risks associated with using it should not be minimized.

For example, Donna Rice Hughes—founder of Enough is Enough, an organization dedicated to making the Internet safer for kids—says that the Internet is a place frequented by a large number of sexual predators. She adds that they use it as a way to exchange information about where to find victims online, how to ensnare them, and how to avoid entrapment by police. Consequently, "the danger to children, whether they are from New York or New Zealand, has drastically increased,"[8] she says, and the risk of interacting with an online predator looms large.

"We should be thankful when kids go online, not afraid."[9]

— Conclusion of an Internet safety study by the Digital Youth Project.

People continue to disagree, however, about just how much alarm is called for and about whether the benefits of the Internet outweigh the risks. A study conducted over three years for the Digital Youth project concluded that the risks have been exaggerated and that "we should be thankful when kids go online, not afraid."[9] In supporting this position, the report notes that the Internet enables young people to acquire knowledge, learn to express themselves better, and become technologically savvy. However, victims of online predation counter that the Internet can also ruin lives, and they point out that minimal risk is not the same as no risk.

Facts

- Every year on January 28, the United States, Canada, and 27 European countries recognize Data Privacy Day, an event designed to raise awareness about the need to protect one's personal information online.

- According to the Family Online Safety Institute, whereas over 40 percent of people in North America use the social networking site Facebook, less than 4 percent of people in Asia do.

- A national analysis by the University of New Hampshire found that the arrests in one year for online sexual predation constitute only 1 percent of all arrests for sex crimes committed against minors.

What Are the Origins of the Online Predator Problem?

Imagine a woman walking down a street alone at night. A strange man approaches, and she realizes he is going to try to talk to her. In most cases, the woman would cross to the other side of the street to avoid the stranger and perhaps walk faster to get away from him as quickly as possible. It is, she will say to herself, the safest thing to do.

Now imagine a woman on the Internet alone at night. A stranger approaches her in an online forum and tries to strike up a conversation. In most cases, the woman will respond to him, a chat session will begin, and one or both might end up revealing highly personal information—information that could be exploited by a cybercriminal.

Letting Down One's Guard

What is it about the Internet that makes people let down their guard when strangers approach? Psychologists studying this issue have found that the nature of the Internet encourages such behavior. In his book *The Psychology of Cyberspace*, psychologist John Suler explains, "It's well known that people say and do things in cyberspace that they wouldn't ordinarily say or do in the face-to-face world. They loosen up, feel more uninhibited, express themselves more openly. Researchers call this the 'disinhibition effect.'"[10]

Suler notes that this effect has both positives and negatives. "It's a double-edged sword," he says.

> Sometimes people share very personal things about themselves. They reveal secret emotions, fears, wishes. Or they show unusual acts of kindness and generosity. We may call this *benign disinhibition*. On the other hand, the disinhibition effect may not be so benign. Out spills rude language and harsh criticisms, anger, hatred, even threats. Or people explore the dark underworld of the internet, places of pornography and violence, places they would never visit in the real world. We might call this *toxic disinhibition*.[11]

Losing One's Self

Researchers studying the psychology of cyberspace have noted several factors that encourage people to behave differently online than they do offline. These include anonymity, invisibility, the lack of authority figures on the Internet, the gamelike quality of computer interactions, and the feeling in some users that talking online is the same as talking to oneself.

In other words, Internet users often see cyberspace as an extension of themselves. This means that the boundary between "me" and "not me" is blurred. According to Suler, this blurring results largely because people immersed in the online world are not engaging all of their senses, as they would in the real world. Consequently, they lose awareness of the physical body—their own, and those of the people with whom they are communicating.

Moreover, because the Internet has a timeless nature that isolates people from the physical world, spending a great deal of time online can produce an altered state of consciousness. This is why many people report that time seems to pass much more quickly when they are using the Internet. It is also why many people say they do not always feel like themselves when they are online. With this feeling can come

"Many kids need nothing more than a keyboard and an Internet connection to get themselves into a world of electronic trouble."[12]

—Frederick S. Lane, in *Cybertraps for the Young.*

false ideas about the nature of other people online, making it difficult to judge whether another individual is a friend or an enemy.

Young and Old

People of all ages can have trouble making judgments about an online stranger's character, but young people often have more trouble maintaining personal boundaries online than adults do. Attorney Frederick S. Lane, an expert in issues related to technology, supports this view in his book *Cybertraps for the Young*, in which he shows that the younger the people involved in a chat, the more likely personal, exploitable information will be shared. He says, "Many kids need nothing more than a keyboard and an Internet connection to get themselves in a world of electronic trouble."[12] In discussing why online predation is such a problem, he points to the fact that "we're handing our children remarkably powerful devices long before they have the wisdom or maturity to understand the consequences of misusing them."[13]

However, even mature people can fall prey to predators. Indeed, studies have shown that seniors are the most at risk of becoming victims of online financial scams. To confirm this, in 2011 the Institute of Criminality in Australia interviewed 120 people who had lost a combined total of 1.4 million dollars due to such scams. They found that nearly half of these victims were over 55 years of age, and that one-third of them had been victimized by strangers they had met on online matchmaking sites. Fifteen had been conned into taking out personal loans to give money to these strangers, and six had mortgaged property in order to do so.

This suggests that the root of the predator problem is not necessarily a lack of maturity but a case of too much trust. Indeed, a 2009 survey by the Nielsen Company found that 70 percent of Internet users trust the recommendations and advice of online strangers. But other studies have shown that without face-to-face contact, people often form wrong impressions about how similar or dissimilar they are to an online stranger. In one such study, anthropologist David Jacobson of Brandeis University interviewed individuals who took an online relationship offline and discovered that the images formed during online interactions were very differ-

Predator Caution

Like everyone else using the Internet, predators cannot be sure of the identities of the people they are communicating with online. However, according to law enforcement authorities, sexual predators are increasingly using digital photos to verify the age and gender of potential victims. Such predators will ask an intended victim to take a digital photograph of him- or herself for immediate transmission to the predator. But first, to be sure the photo has not been prepared in advance by police seeking to trick sexual offenders, the predator will dictate exactly how the subject should stand in the photo, and perhaps also say what kind or color of clothing the person should wear. The predator will not ask for any poses or clothing that might be considered provocative, though, because then the request could be considered evidence of a sexual solicitation And the predator's intent at this point is not to get sexually suggestive pictures, but to verify that the person sending the photo is a minor and not with law enforcement. (Many predators know that law enforcement agencies cannot use minors to contact predators.)

ent from reality. A person pictured as very short might be very tall, for example, and someone who seemed confident might actually be shy. Jacobson reports that most of the people he interviewed were mistaken about the appearance and nature of their Internet friends, and he quotes one man as saying, "It's draining when you realize how different people are from what they project online."[14]

A Need to Believe

Misperceptions, then, are also to blame when it comes to being deceived online—and when this is the case, often the victim wants to believe in the misperception. Diane Carbo, a nurse who specializes in helping the elderly, explains that many scams are based on people's need to trust someone who is telling them what they want to hear. "It feels good when someone is telling you nice things," she says, and this is especially true for people who want to believe that they have "truly and finally, after all the loneliness and social isolation, found someone to connect with."[15]

According to Les Henderson, an expert on financial fraud, scammers have told police that their ideal victim is a lonely, isolated older adult who has no contact with family members. Such people are particularly vulnerable to falling prey to romance-related scams. Carbo reports, "Victims soon find themselves entangled by emotion, believing the scammer needs money for this or that, and end up broke, humiliated and devastated by the discovery of the con. That doesn't mean the victim is an idiot, it simply means that the person wanted to believe he or she had found happiness. It can happen to anyone in the right situation."[16]

In fact, scam artists are typically very good at assessing the emotional needs of their victims. Studies have shown that the most successful online scams are those that take advantage of what scammers would call human weaknesses. These include a desire to be liked, loved, famous or wealthy; guilt over having too much or not giving enough to the less fortunate (in cases where a victim is convinced to send money to a supposed cancer victim, for example); and a big ego, which can cause victims not to consult experts before investing money. A know-it-all attitude can also cause people to ignore good advice about how to protect themselves and their computers from online predation.

However, letting down one's guard in online social forums is more often the result of carelessness. As users of such forums become more and more deeply invested in the community of the forum, they can forget that their conversations there can be viewed by countless others not involved in the forum. That is, the forum begins to feel intimate rather than vast, as though participants are just like neighbors chatting over a backyard fence. This feeling can encourage a naïveté about the type of people who might be lurking online, making it seem as though everyone is a true friend.

The Beginnings of the Internet

A naïveté about online dangers has existed ever since the Internet was first made available to the general public. Initially, only academics, scientists, and the military used the Internet, and the popular belief is that it was developed in 1969 by the US Pentagon, perhaps with help from scientists and academics, to ensure that top government officials could still communicate with one another after a nuclear attack. Most historians dismiss this view, though they disagree on just when, how, and by whom the Internet was invented. They also disagree on how the Internet should be defined, but the most basic definition is that it is a worldwide system of interconnected computers and networks.

The Internet of the twenty-first century arose from the development of the personal computer, the high-speed modem, and the World Wide Web in the last three decades of the twentieth century. Beginning in the 1970s, personal computers were sold at prices that middle-class people could afford (the first, the Altair 8800, was sold in 1975 for $379), and high-speed modems transmitted digital information over telephone lines fast enough to allow for real-time online communication in chat rooms, social networking sites, and similar forums. The World Wide Web made

The user-friendly Internet of the twenty-first century was once a tool used mainly by scientists, academics, and the military. Today it boasts an infinite number of resources, tools, and services including websites for online retailers such as Amazon (the business's warehouse is shown here).

the Internet user-friendly, allowed people to post pictures and music online, and inspired the creation of merchant websites where people could buy and sell things online.

Downsides of Technology

However, each advance came with a downside. The affordability, speed of communication, and user-friendly features of personal computers made them just as attractive to criminals as to law-abiding citizens. The ability to share pictures allowed sexual predators to expose potential victims, many of them adolescents, to pornographic images. The creation of chat rooms and similar forums gave predators a place to gain the trust of their eventual victims, and the use of computers to conduct financial transactions provided new opportunities to steal money.

Over time, more and more personal information became available online for everyone to view. Sometimes a person would put his or her own information on the Internet; other times the source was a friend, a relative, an employer or someone else. Marketers often shared their databases on the Internet, for example, and public records such as court documents, county and state records, voter registration, and marriage licenses also found their way online. In any case, once such information is online, it can be difficult or impossible to remove. For example, a person might want to keep a home address private but will be unable to find and delete all appearances of it on the Internet.

> "[Before the Internet,] your privacy was protected from leaking out beyond the walls of your small town."[7]
>
> — Richard Guerry, founder and executive director of the Institute for Responsible Online and Cell-Phone Communication.

Redefining Community

Richard Guerry, founder and executive director of the Institute for Responsible Online and Cell-Phone Communication, notes that decades ago home addresses and phone numbers were public information too, but geography generally limited who had access to them. That is, most people who could find out a person's address were friends and neighbors in the same town, not strangers on the other side of the world. This was true of other personal information as well. Guerry reports that "the geographical and technological limitations of earlier times often caused [small] towns to be very isolated from one another. While your mayor would stop by for weekly cups of coffee and your butcher knew your Sunday order by heart, it was also very unlikely that you would know much about the lives of people outside of your own little town." He adds that this lifestyle provided a benefit: "knowing that your privacy was protected from leaking out beyond the walls of your small town."[17]

Moreover, Guerry says, whereas in the 1940s information took a long time to spread even in a small town of 500 people, today it takes only a few seconds for this to happen, and instead of reaching just a few hundred people, the information might reach billions. Consequently, he says, "The small town *on* earth is now the small town *of* earth."[18] In other words, the world's geopolitical boundaries are collapsing just as surely as the personal boundaries of online users.

"Sex offenders who target juveniles are a diverse group that cannot be accurately characterized with one-dimensional labels."[19]

— Conclusion of a study conducted by the Crimes Against Children Research Center of the University of New Hampshire.

Taken Unaware

Guerry and others note that in the early years of the Internet, most users were unaware of the potential dangers associated with going online. Excited by the new venues for communication and commerce that the Internet presented, adults went online with an innocence that made them easy prey for financial scammers. Parents also allowed their children to go online with minimal supervision, and this led to the first reported cases of sexual predation connected to children using social networking sites.

Among the most significant of these cases was that of George Stanley Burdynski Jr., a 10-year-old boy from Brentwood, Maryland, who disappeared on May 24, 1993. That afternoon at approximately 3:30 p.m. he left home on his bicycle to visit an adult friend, Robert Violet, at the house of the man's mother. Violet claimed that George never showed up, but others said they saw the boy in front of the house. In either case, George was spotted riding his bicycle near the house at about 8:30 p.m., the last time anyone saw him.

The next day, Violet and George's father searched for the missing boy. They found a piece of the bicycle—a spare rim that Burdynski had tied to his handlebars—three blocks from Violet's mother's house, but nothing else turned up. However, agents of the Federal Bureau of Investigation (FBI), working with Maryland law enforcement officers, gathered enough evidence to suspect that George's disappearance was connected to the activities of three men involved in child pornography.

Child Exploitation

Specifically, Steven Leak (also known as Bruce Leak), James A. Kowalski Jr., and Joseph Lynch had been talking to young boys online, trying to convince them to meet with the men in person. During these meetings, the men would force the boys to pose for pornographic pictures that would then be posted on a private on-line "bulletin board" viewed by pedophiles, people who receive sexual gratification from looking at child pornography and/or having sex with children. The weekend before George disappeared, these three men had allegedly sexually abused two of his friends, and George had once visited Lynch's home with these boys.

The three men were never charged with anything related to the Burdynki case, although they were convicted of abusing others, and George has never been found. However his case inspired the FBI to launch a major investigation into Internet child exploitation. In addition, because of massive publicity related to the case, it made many parents aware for the first time of just how dangerous the Internet could be for children.

Predator Profiles

Once law enforcement agencies started directing resources toward investigating online predation, they learned that the problem is highly complex. In particular, they found that it is extremely difficult to identify the people who cause the problem—so difficult, in fact, that some cybercrime experts believe that the term "predator" is not accurate. For example, the University of New Hampshire researchers say that "the term 'predator' can mischaracterize some offenders . . . by giving the impression that these are uniformly highly motivated, repetitive, and aggressive sex offenders. In reality, sex offenders who target juveniles are a diverse group that cannot be accurately characterized with one-dimensional labels."[19]

In fact, many experts disagree on what a "typical" offender might be like, and members of the general public have many misperceptions about the types of people who become predators. Most people believe that the majority of sexual predators are older, white males, often with a history of offline sexual offenses against young children. In actuality, predators can be of any race, and an increasing number of online sexual predators are teens or young

Sleep Deprivation

Some researchers believe that the reason behind much of the careless behavior and bad decisions that lead to online victimization are caused by sleep deprivation. Habitual computer users can stay up late into the night searching websites, participating in chat rooms, and engaging in other Internet-related activities even though they have to get up early the next morning. In addition, many find that using the computer right before bed will lead to problems falling asleep or will disrupt their sleep patterns. A 2010 report by the Sleep Disorder Center at JFK Medical Center in Edison, New Jersey, reveals that four out of five teenagers who use technological devices prior to sleep can develop insomnia and/or many other problems, including attention deficit disorder. Over time, the loss of sleep can affect judgment as well. A study conducted at the Rush Medical College in Chicago, Illinois, found that people with less than four hours of sleep a night made over twice the errors of those who received over seven hours a night. Other studies have shown that sleep-deprived people can also react inappropriately or experience inappropriate emotions.

adults. (By some estimates, in 2000 roughly one-fourth of online sexual predators were 18 to 25 years of age, and in 2006 nearly half were.) Moreover, a University of New Hampshire survey of 2,500 law enforcement agencies found that only 6 percent of arrested online predators were registered sex offenders. Most were white males, however, although the number of minority offenders is growing; whereas in 2000, 10 percent of arrested online predators were members of minority groups, in 2006 that number rose to 16 percent.

According to the New Hampshire researchers and Michele L. Ybarra of *Internet Solutions for Kids, Inc.*, these misguided notions about the nature of online predators have led to well-meaning but ineffective approaches to addressing the predator problem. They explain:

> The publicity about online "predators" who prey on naïve children using trickery and violence is largely inaccurate. Internet sex crimes involving adults and juveniles more often fit a model of statutory rape—adult offenders who meet, develop relationships with, and openly seduce underage teenagers—than a model of forcible sexual assault or pedophilic child molesting. This is a serious problem, but one that requires approaches different from those in current prevention messages emphasizing parental control and the dangers of divulging personal information.[20]

Need for Caution?

But many Internet safety experts are opposed to the notion that parental control measures and warnings should be discarded, believing that a lack of these things will cause predation to rise. To support their view, they cite government reports that one in seven young people is approached online by a stranger with motivations related to sexual exploitation, and they argue that young people need guidance on how to deal with such situations. Consequently many Internet safety websites stress the importance of parents having rules for teens to follow while online.

For example, the InternetSafetyRules.net website says:

Scores of members [at social networking sites] including children and teenagers post photos and pictures of themselves online. This can of course be dangerous, especially when other personal information is divulged too, like address, city, town, school etc. What will make online predators stop making use of such information to work on? Let your child understand the possible deep implications or consequences of all these. Let them be confronted with the question—"if a predator turns up at their door while they are alone, due to the information provided online, how will they like it!?" The fear factor should work for the good of your child making them follow the internet safety rules.[21]

The New Hampshire researchers disagree with the view that social networking sites are dangerous, even though they admit that 33 percent of children and teens victimized by online predation met their predator at such a site. This statistic, they argue, is

Law enforcement agencies nationwide are increasing their investigations into the activities of online predators. Pictured behind this Pennsylvania investigator are mug shots of online predators.

misleading because social networking sites are so popular. That is, more young people are victimized on such sites simply because so many young people use such sites. The researchers report that in 2006 an estimated 55 percent of young people ages 12 to 17, roughly 14 million youth, used social networking sites, and they state that such sites are statistically no more dangerous than places young people frequent offline.

Look to the Victims

Many people would disagree that the online world is no more dangerous than the offline world, particularly considering people's tendency to let down their guard when approached by strangers on the Internet. They also note that the New Hampshire researchers based their conclusions on mail surveys of law enforcement agencies that addressed arrests made during only two 12-month periods, July 1, 2000, through July 30, 2001, and the calendar year of 2006. The researchers believe that this representative sampling is enough to draw valid conclusions concerning online predators and their victims—but they admit that more study is needed to confirm these conclusions.

Still, psychologists generally agree with the New Hampshire study's conclusion that anticrime experts would have greater success in combating predation if they focused more on the prey than on the predator. Victims tend to share certain psychological and behavioral traits, and if these traits can be identified prior to victimization, then anticrime education efforts can be targeted to the population where victimhood originates. Within this point of origin, many experts argue, lies the key to keeping people safe online.

Facts

- Studies conducted by Internet safety software companies have indicated that nearly three-fourths of online solicitations occur while the victim is using a home computer as opposed to a computer at a school, library, or other public place.

- Surveys indicate that on average, teens spend roughly 31 hours per week online.

- According to the Girl Scout Research Institute, over 90 percent of teenage girls say they have not told their parents about an online sexual solicitation or bullying incident for fear it would lead to a ban on Internet use.

- According to the US Justice Department, terrorists and other criminals often conduct business at Internet cafés, which are coffee houses, and similar places that offer Internet access.

- Studies by experts in psychology and human development indicate that a majority of teenagers are more comfortable expressing their emotions online than elsewhere.

Who Is Most at Risk from Online Predators?

In November 2011, 27-year-old Cameron Stuart Hore of Christchurch, New Zealand, was arrested and charged with sexually exploiting minors. His victims were boys, some as young as 11, whom he found by posing as a teenage girl named Sarah Ruddenklau on two social network sites, Facebook and MSN Messenger. Hore lured the boys with a photograph of "Sarah," an attractive young woman whom police have yet to identify.

Once a potential victim began exchanging messages with Hore, believing him to be a girl, he would gradually gain the victim's trust and e-mail the boy nude pictures of "Sarah." Hore would then ask the victim to expose himself and/or perform sexual acts in front of a webcam, a camera that allowed Hore—still pretending to be "Sarah"—to view the victim's actions online. By this point, Hore could determine whether a victim was especially trusting and/or sexually adventurous, and he persuaded these victims to meet in person with a man named Dan McPherson, another of Hore's false identities. During these meetings, "McPherson" would convince or pay the boys to allow him to perform sexual acts on them.

Escalating Actions

Hore's gradual gaining of his victims' trust is a process known as grooming, whereby predators persuade potential victims to become actual victims. According to the American Psychological Association, most online sexual predators engage in grooming, taking the time to develop a relationship with their victims prior to taking action. In this way, they often convince their victims to view the predation as a romance or sexual adventure.

Typically, the escalating actions that mark the progression to victim begin with exposing the victim to sexual remarks and/or visual images. The victim might also be shown disturbing pornography. After this, the victim is coaxed into sharing photographs of him- or herself online, perhaps along with personal and possibly sexually charged information. Finally, victims might be persuaded to meet with the predator in person. Such a meeting might simply involve nonviolent sexual acts, or it might result in the victim being imprisoned, raped, and/or murdered.

Young People Without Supervision

In seeking out victims for grooming, predators often favor young people who spend much of their free time online. Internet safety expert Michael Ryan, who has developed software to help parents monitor their children's online actions, explains: "Predators have little chance to groom a child for future exploitation if that child is rarely online or is online at various times of the day. Children who do not have a lot of activities outside of school tend to be online longer and at the same times of day compared to those children who have lots of activities. These children are more often targeted by internet predators."[22]

Ryan points out that Internet predators target youth who do not hesitate to speak to strangers. Predators specifically look for lonely young people from dysfunctional homes because these young people are more likely to want to form a close relationship with an Internet "friend." In addition, he says, predators often look for potential victims who have access to webcams and/or digital cameras, since sharing pornographic images is a large part of their victimization. Young people who communicate by e-mail are less likely to be targeted because their computers typically save e-mails automatically, thereby providing evidence that could later be used to convict their predators.

"Predators have little chance to groom a child for future exploitation if that child is rarely online or is online at various times of the day."[22]

— Michael Ryan, Internet safety expert.

Sexually Curious

Another factor in choosing victims is sexual curiosity. Ryan explains: "Internet predators seem to favor victims between the ages of 12–15. These are the ages [when] children are discovering their own sexuality and independence, and also the ages where they are most likely to be conned into meeting with a stranger without telling their parents. Younger and older children are also solicited, but as a whole tend to be harder targets."[23]

Sexual curiosity is also what draws teenage boys to interact with online sexual predators, who are predominantly male. According to a study by the University of New Hampshire, "Boys who are gay or are questioning their sexuality may be more susceptible to Internet-initiated sex crimes than other populations. Researchers found boys were the victims in nearly one-quarter of criminal cases, and most cases included the fact that suggested victims were gay or questioning their sexuality."[24]

Young people exploring their sexuality are also more likely to solicit sexual conversations in chat rooms. In his book *Cybertraps for the Young*, Frederick S. Lane provides an example of this behavior by sharing an excerpt from a session in a teen chat room. This excerpt includes vulgar language as well as comments like, "girl looking for girl or guy," "any cute girls wanna chat?" and "Hey, 17 year old male from so cali (sandiego actually) im sweet-caring honest, and not a perv or freak im reall chill, and outgoing, and funny (so ive been told) lookin to get to know locals and new friends and meet genuine people so hit me up."[25]

The chat room where these comments were made included over 150 other participants, along with an unknown number of people who were reading the comments but not participating in any conversations. Consequently the teens soliciting responses—often using vulgar or sexually charged language—had no way of knowing exactly what kind of people they were reaching out to. Some might have been the teenage girls or boys they were seeking, but others might have been adult males with a record of committing sexual offenses.

In many cases, teens talking this way in chat rooms are well aware that they are taking a risk. Psychologists say this is because

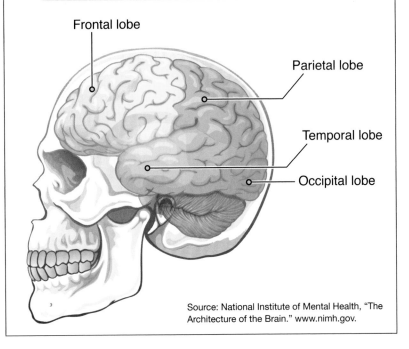

The Teenage Brain

From a purely physiological standpoint, teenagers have immature brains. This stage of development helps to explain the high emotions and risk-taking behaviors commonly exhibited by teens. Behavior is controlled by the frontal lobe of the brain, which does not reach maturity until after adolescence. This might help explain why teens are more at risk than some other age groups on the Internet.

Frontal lobe

Parietal lobe

Temporal lobe

Occipital lobe

Source: National Institute of Mental Health, "The Architecture of the Brain." www.nimh.gov.

teenagers are predisposed to take risks because of their brain development at that stage of life. According to Temple University professor of psychology Laurence Steinberg, who has studied teenage risk-taking behavior, having an immature brain means that "kids have much more difficulty controlling their impulses and regulating their behavior than adults do."[26]

Child and adolescent psychiatrist Jay Giedd, who has performed brain-imaging research as part of a study of teenage brains for the National Institute of Mental Health (NIMH), agrees with this assessment, saying that puberty is the time when the brain is most predisposed to encourage risk taking. "That is when the balance is tipped most in favor of high emotions and risk taking," he says. "The key parts of the brain involved in controlling impulses and risky behavior don't really reach maturity until about age 25."[27]

Steinberg says this is why education programs designed to prevent teens from engaging in dangerous behaviors often do not work. "I don't want to suggest that we should stop educating teens about these dangers, but we shouldn't kid ourselves. Just because we are giving kids the facts, that doesn't mean that we are changing their behavior."[28]

Many experts on brain development believe that teens as a whole have a predisposition toward taking risks. But Internet security expert Larry Magid argues that only some teens are risk takers. "Most kids are pretty careful when it comes to Internet safety," he says, "but a small percentage of teens take unnecessary risks that could lead to sexual solicitations and other dangers. Based on what we know about teenage risk taking, it is likely that the same kids who are abusing drugs or driving while under the influence are the same ones who are taking extraordinary risks online."[29]

Darker Motives

Sometimes, though, teens who believe they are taking one kind of risk are actually taking another, because sexual gratification is not the only thing an online predator might want. For example, in 2011 an 18-year-old man became friends with 22-year-old Rebecca Chandler through online chats. Over time, she made the man think she was interested in having sex with him, so he traveled from his home in Phoenix, Arizona, to Milwaukee, Wisconsin, in order to meet with her in person. However, Chandler apparently had not been grooming the man for sexual purposes but for satanic purposes. While this might not be typical of online predators, it does illustrate the dangers of meeting online contacts.

Specifically, after the victim arrived at the woman's apartment,

Chandler and her roommate, 20-year-old Raven Larrabee, tied him up and kept him there for two days. Then Chandler apparently had sex with him while Larrabee cut and stabbed him more than 300 times on his back, face, arms, legs, and neck. The women later claimed that the man's wounds were caused by sexual play that got out of hand, but the police noted that the crime scene was littered with books on satanism, the occult, necromancy, and werewolves, including at least one that featured ritual stabbing. They believe the two women decided to lure a man to their apartment so they could sacrifice him in an occult ritual.

Financial Motives

Another motive for online predators is greed. Financial predators target people who not only have money but who are also careless about how they conduct their monetary transactions online and/or are too trusting of strangers while engaging in electronic commerce (e-commerce). Typical victims also spend a great deal of time online, often to stave off boredom and/or loneliness.

Many elderly people, especially those who are housebound due to health problems, fit this profile. Consequently, according to both the American Association of Retired Persons (AARP) and the FBI, seniors are especially vulnerable to financial fraud. In addition, some financial predators specifically target senior citizens because older people tend to own their own homes and have savings and good credit. Seniors also tend to be more polite and trusting in their interactions with strangers because of the way people of their generation were raised.

The AARP, reporting in 2011 on its year-long study of seniors victimized by financial predators, also shows that seniors engage in behaviors that put them at greater risk for being contacted by online predators. Specifically, they often enter drawings and contests for free prizes, attend free-lunch seminars about services like investment management, and/or accept free trips that come with sales pitches, all of which require them to provide their e-mail address. With this address, financial predators can send potential victims fake e-mails from reputable companies that convince these victims to provide sensitive information like user names,

Cyberstalking

Secretly following and spying on an intended victim before assaulting him or her is called "stalking." Many people think the term *cyberstalking* applies to the use of a computer to find or track the intended victim's whereabouts. However, in many places the courts define cyberstalking as the use of the Internet to harass another person online by repeatedly making threats, false accusations, or similar comments against that person to the point where it causes severe emotional harm. This definition of cyberstalking does not necessarily require the offender to follow a person around the Internet; that is, the offender need not make the threats, accusations, or comments on more than one website. For example, in 2011 a 15-year-old girl in Rhode Island was charged with cyberstalking because she used a fake Facebook page to severely ridicule a girl with a birth defect.

passwords, and credit card details. E-mails also offer a way for scammers to convince victims to pay fees in advance for things the victim will never receive.

Among the victims studied by the AARP, advance-fee frauds—when the victim pays money up front thinking it is a processing fee for a loan, investment return, or lottery winnings—were the most common. Other common scams involved convincing victims to "buy" fake products and services related to health care or other issues of importance to seniors. But the study also noted that only 25 percent of all the victims in their study reported the crime to law enforcement.

Many anticrime experts have noted that seniors severely underreport such crimes. The FBI explains, "Older Americans are less likely to report a fraud because they don't know who to report it to, are too ashamed at having been scammed, or don't know they have been scammed. Elderly victims may not report crimes, for example, because they are concerned that relatives may think the victims no longer have the mental capacity to take care of their own financial affairs."[30] Just based on the number of crimes being reported, however, experts have been able to determine that financial fraud is the fasting growing form of victimization among the elderly.

Young Adults Also Targeted

Studies also suggest that online financial predators are increasingly finding success among teenagers as well. In affluent countries, one-fourth of this age group report having access to credit cards, either their own or cards provided by parents, and half of these teens report having used them to make online purchases. Consequently scammers are coming up with new ways to target young people.

In fact, in September 2010 journalist Melissa Singer of the *Sydney Morning Herald* reported that because financial predators are now shifting their focus to teenagers, Australian victims ages 18–24 lose more money than all other age groups: an average of $1,619 as compared to $1,000. Singer suggests this is because, according to a survey by the Internet security company VeriSign, 69 percent of teens transfer money over the Internet without making sure they are on a secure site where personal information cannot be seen by others. Singer quotes Mark Gregory, an expert on computer networks, as saying that this practice is "equivalent to holding [personal information] up on a board in the middle of a supermarket, but it's worse than that. You can take the board and go home, but on the internet you can't."[31]

As with seniors, the most common scams currently victimizing teenagers are advance-fee frauds, which con people into sending money in advance for things they will never receive. The "bait" for teen victims is most typically related to scholarships, student loans, careers, jobs, and teen-appealing "prizes." For example, victims are told they have won a "free" notebook computer but must first pay for shipping if they want to receive it. Job scams require "prospective employees" to pay up-front "application" fees or "training" fees. Scholarship scams charge students to provide them with information about college funding, then send them a

Nigerian Scammers

The country of Nigeria has been connected to many advance-fee scams. In fact, one of these is so tied to Nigeria that it is known in many places as the Nigerian Advance Fee Scam, or internationally as the 4-1-9 fraud because 419 is the section of Nigeria's criminal code that the scam violates. In this scam, the predator sends an e-mail to the victim claiming to be an official of a foreign government, usually Nigeria, who has embezzled money and needs help getting it out of the country. To do this, the "official" says, he would like to wire it to the victim's bank account, then transfer the money elsewhere—and in exchange for the victim allowing his bank account to act as a way station, the victim will supposedly receive a generous percentage of the money being transferred. Willing victims are then asked to provide personal banking information and/or to pay certain fees to facilitate the money transfer, thereby giving the predator the opportunity to defraud them.

list of scholarships that can be found free elsewhere or is worthless. Talent scams tell teens that they can become models or actors by coming in for an audition—after they pay a small fee required to book an appointment for a meeting that will never happen.

A Well-Publicized Case

Another common scam that financial predators can tailor to a particular audience is the too-good-to-be-true deal, whereby an item is advertised as being for sale at an unbelievably low price. The victim must pay for the item in advance, however, and of course it never arrives. In a related scam, the victim is selling an item, and the "buyer" convinces the seller to ship the item in advance of payment. The seller never receives the money.

An example of a seller being scammed by a financial predator appeared on the reality TV show *Teen Mom* on MTV, in September 2010. Teenage mom Farrah listed her car for sale online and received an offer of $5,000 plus another $3,000 for shipping. The buyer then sent Farrah a check for $8,000, telling her to immediately wire the shipping money to a certain account managed by a third party who would make the transportation arrangements. Farrah deposited the check in her bank account, made the wire transfer of funds, and subsequently found out that the check was no good, which meant that the wired money was deducted from Farrah's savings.

Consumer psychologist Kit Yarrow argues that the *Teen Mom* case illustrates her position that members of the current generation of young people are more likely to fall for scams than other groups. She says, "I think Gen Y's optimistic nature leaves them more vulnerable to scams. Compared to other generations, Gen Y feels like things will turn out well and imagines the best. This makes them less vigilant in general."[32]

Dating Scams

But other groups of people can demonstrate a naïve optimism as well, and this is especially true among those who fall for financial scams connected to romance and dating. Such people can be so desperate to find love that they believe whatever they are told about their potential mate's background and overlook warning signs that all might not be as it seems. Moreover, financial predators who engage in "sweetheart scams" often find victims via reputable dating sites that make people feel safe about developing relationships there. For example, Julie Ferguson, executive director of a company that tracks scams for online retailers, says that many scammers target users of sites for Christian singles because people are less suspicious of others on such sites. Ferguson reports: "When you are meeting someone else on a Christian site, you think you are safe."[33]

Another component of this scam that makes it difficult for victims to believe they are being duped is that sweetheart scammers often take months to develop a relationship with a potential

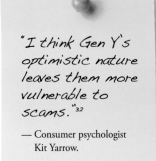

"I think Gen Y's optimistic nature leaves them more vulnerable to scams."[32]

— Consumer psychologist Kit Yarrow.

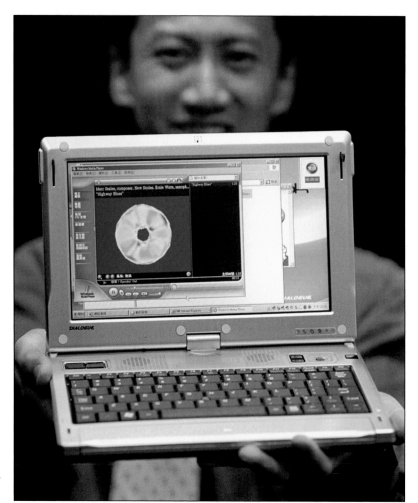

A common online scam, typically sent by text or e-mail, congratulates a user on winning a free notebook computer (such as the one pictured). To collect the so-called prize, the user must pay for shipping and other costs. Once these costs are paid, the notebook mysteriously fails to arrive.

victim before striking. According to the FBI, a scammer might even romance a victim for as long as a year before deciding to finish off the fraud. At this point, the scammer starts asking for gifts, or "loans" of money, or the favor of cashing a money order.

Forty-six-year-old Theresa Smalley offers an example of the latter. Smalley, who shared her story with MSNBC news in order to warn others about romance scams, cashed two money orders, at $900 each, for a man with whom she had been in an online relationship for two months. This man, "Richie," had claimed that he was from Milford, Connecticut, but was working in the African country of Nigeria on a construction project. He told Smalley that his US boss had been paying him in money orders and that he was having trouble cashing them in a foreign country. After Smalley agreed to help, he sent her the money orders and she cashed them and wired him the funds. He then asked her to cash another money order, and she complied.

Shortly thereafter, her bank called her to tell her that the money orders had been doctored so that they looked like they were worth more than they really were; each one had a value of only $20. This meant that when Smalley cashed the money order at her bank, the bank gave her money she wasn't entitled to. "The bank told me I was responsible for that money," she says. "I had to pay them $2,700, which was everything I had. I was devastated. I felt like my whole world had fallen apart."[34]

Blindsided

By this time, Smalley had been corresponding with "Richie" for four months, and he had sent her gifts of candy and a teddy bear—a practice akin to grooming by sexual predators. Experts in dating scams say such gifts are typically bought with a stolen credit card number. Smalley had also seen a reassuring photo of the person she thought was "Richie"—a man about her age who looked friendly and was hugging a cat. This too is similar to the approach that sexual predators take—creating a false persona to lure victims.

"Never in my wildest dreams would I have ever known that this is all part of an elaborate online scam,"[35] Smalley says. Many targets of online sexual predators are just as blindsided by their victimization as Smalley was. Moreover, both kinds of victims can be so traumatized by their experiences that they have trouble trusting anyone in the future.

Facts

- When a teen, while talking to other teens in a chat room, types a code like POS ("Parent Over Shoulder") to shut down a conversation that adults would not like, lurking predators can tell that the teen is willing to keep secrets from his or her parents.

- The term "phishing" refers to forged or fake e-mails that falsely claim to be from a reputable company in order to con the victim into providing personal, sensitive information, such as passwords or a social security number.

- Unsolicited bulk e-mail, widely known as spam, is one of the most common ways that financial predators initiate contact with potential victims.

- According to a recent study by the Media Awareness Network, when asked how long it took for them to feel they could trust someone they had just met online, teenage girls gave answers ranging from just 15 minutes to two weeks.

- According to a 2010 study by McAfee, Inc., girls are more likely to chat with strangers online than boys.

CHAPTER THREE

Are Internet Dangers Exaggerated?

I n early 2012 Lisa H. Warren of Massachusetts, blogged on Hubpages.com about the need to convince children not to talk to *any* strangers, no matter how nice they might seem to be. She reports that she stressed this rule with her own children after they talked to a real estate agent who approached them in a car. The story she tells to prove that they learned the lesson, however, shows how difficult it is for parents to teach their kids about "stranger danger" without going overboard:

> I once needed to use a free-standing ATM, which had three glass walls around it. I parked, truly, six feet from the floor-to-ceiling glass wall and told my three kids I would be "two seconds" and was going to lock the doors of the car. I told them I could see them from the ATM but still told them not to unlock the doors for anyone. I brought the keys with me. I rushed into the ATM, keeping an eye on the car at all times, and then rushed out. Rather than bothering with the key, I signaled to my kids to unlock the door for me. They wouldn't. I used the key, got in, and said, "When I said not to unlock the car I didn't mean don't unlock it for me." My very young son said, "How did we know it wasn't someone disguised as you?"[36]

Since the children had watched their mother leave the car and come back again, their concern about "stranger danger" clearly outweighed common sense. But what about on the Internet, where criminals can easily disguise themselves as friends? Some say it is vitally important to stay away from all strangers there. But others argue that this degree of caution is unnecessary given the odds of encountering an online predator.

Percentages of Contact

According to a study reported in the *Journal of Adolescent Health* in 2010, the majority of Internet-associated sex crimes against young people are initiated in chat rooms. However, the same study showed that only 18 percent of them use chat rooms, suggesting that most young people are at a low risk of encountering a sexual predator online. Moreover, according to an earlier study conducted by the Rochester Institute of Technology, only 9 percent of students in grades 7–9 have accepted an online invitation to meet a stranger in person; 14 percent in grades 10–12 have done so; and 10 percent of students in grades 7–9 and 14 percent in grades 10–12 have asked someone online to meet them in person. This too suggests that most adolescents are at low risk of being victimized by an online sexual predator.

Studies have also shown that in most cases, online sexual solicitations—instances where one person tries to get another person to say or do something of a sexual nature—are not terribly disturbing to teens. Anywhere from 66 percent to 75 percent, depending on the study, report that they were not particularly upset by the solicitation and considered it mild. Of the remainder, fewer than half report being distressed by the encounter and less than 5 percent say they were frightened by it.

Minimizing Experiences

It is likely, however, that victims are minimizing the seriousness and number of their encounters, given the embarrassing nature of the subject and some teens' admissions about their online behavior. According to a study by Internet security technology company McAfee, more than half of teens say that their parents do not know everything they do online, one-third admit to hiding their Internet activities from their parents either most or all of the time, and more

Trust

The release of the 2010 movie *Trust* caused great concern among parents who saw the film or advertisements for it. It depicts a 14-year-old girl who befriends a man in an online chat room thinking he is 16 years old. Over a period of three months she falls in love with the person she believes him to be and agrees to meet him at a local mall, where she finds out he is in his thirties. He convinces her that their age difference means nothing because they are in love, and he charms her into going with him to a hotel, where he rapes her while secretly filming their sexual activity.

Promoted as being based on a true story, the movie made this rare scenario seem like a common one, thereby drawing criticism from experts charged with educating parents and teachers about the actual risks connected to online predation. Some of these experts participated in efforts to combat the movie's message by sending correct information about predation to educators nationwide.

than half of 16- to 17-year-olds say they share personal information online. In addition, 12 percent of all teens say they have given their cell phone numbers to people they know only from their online activities. Other studies indicate that roughly the same percentage of teens confess to having visited a pornographic website at least once, and 5 percent admit to having talked about sex with strangers online.

Another important statistic related to teen secrecy concerns how aware potential victims are of a sexual predator's intent. According to researchers at the University of New Hampshire, 80 percent of sexual offenders who first encountered their victims online were, at some point before meeting with a victim in person, very clear about their intentions, and only 5 percent pretended to be a teenager rather than an adult. That is, most sex crimes that begin with Internet contact between an adult male predator and a

teen involve a predator who is open about his age and his interest in sex. This means that while the teen might not have been aware upon initial online contact that he or she was dealing with an adult predator, this fact became obvious prior to face-to-face contact, sometime during the process whereby the predator gained the victim's trust. The researchers also say that no force is usually involved in the resulting sexual contact offline, and often the offender is a young adult rather than an older one.

Age of Predator

In fact, according to the Internet Safety Technical Task Force, formed in February 2008 as a joint effort by 49 state attorneys general to determine how to improve children's online safety, most people who use the Internet to attempt to solicit sex or initiate off-line sexual encounters with children or teens are between the ages of 18 and 21. As a result of its research, the task force concluded that "actual threats that youth may face appear to be different than the threats most people imagine."[37] Larry Magid cites this difference in support of his contention that Internet safety risks are exaggerated, implying that younger predators are less to be feared.

Others say that this position is ridiculous because being victimized is no less devastating when the perpetrator is 21 instead of 41. However, the University of New Hampshire researchers argue that the concept of online sexual predation as most frequently involving two young people is far less disturbing than the idea, promoted by the media, that it mostly involves older men—probably repeat sex offenders—who prey on young children. Such misinformation, they suggest, will keep society from dealing with the predator problem in ways that will actually reduce predation. The researchers also note that the media present the online predator problem as a new form of child abuse, when in fact, it is the same as the offline predator problem. "Although a new medium for communication is involved, the nonforcible sex crimes that predominate as offenses against youths online are not particularly new or uncommon."[38]

> "Actual threats that youth may face appear to be different than the threats most people imagine."[37]
>
> — Internet Safety Technical Task Force.

Flawed Definitions

These researchers and others have noted another problem related to the age of the person victimized by online predation: The legal definition of a minor can vary from place to place. In some states, it is illegal to have sex with a person under the age of 16; in others, the age of consent might be anywhere from 14 to 18. Most states attempt to exempt peer relationships by mandating that the offender be above a certain age or that the age difference between the two people involved in the sexual act be more than a certain number of years. But in some states, a young person slightly over the age of consent can be convicted as an offender for having sex with another young person slightly under the age of consent. In Arizona, for example, where the age of consent is 18 and there is no close-in-age exception, a 19-year-old can be prosecuted for having sex with an 17-year-old unless the two are married.

Flawed definitions are also a problem when it comes to research studies. One of the best examples of this is associated with a CBS News report in 2005 and an ABC News report in 2006. Both cited an alarming statistic regarding online predation that has often been repeated since then, including on the ProtectKids.com website: that one in five young people has been approached by a sexual predator while online. But according to the Committee for Skeptical Inquiry (CSI), this oft-cited statistic can be traced back to a Department of Justice study that used an extremely broad definition of online predation.

Specifically, the study defined sexual solicitation by a predator as any request of a sexual nature. That is, someone would be considered a sexual predator for asking a teenager to talk about sex, engage in a sexual activity, or provide personal information of a sexual nature. The predator could be an adult or a teenager, although in the case of teenagers, the sexual request had to be unwanted to be considered solicitation for purposes of the study. Still, skeptic and media critic Benjamin Radford says that given the study's definition, "one teen asking another teen if he or she is a virgin—or got lucky with a recent date—could be considered 'sexual solicitation.'"[39]

Nearly half of the "sexual solicitations" in the study involved "predators" who were teenagers, and none of these solicitations actually resulted in any physical sexual contact. Radford therefore considers the study, and the resulting "one in five" statistic that it provides, to be flawed. He contends that what it called predation was just "the equivalent of teen flirting."[40] He adds that when the study considered only possible predators who engaged in truly worrisome online behavior, such as trying to coerce a teen into meeting them in person or sending a teen unrequested gifts, that statistic dropped to only 3 percent.

Media Distortion

Radford has also criticized reporters and politicians for making misleading statements about online predation. As a classic case of media distortion, he cites an April 2005 television report in which CBS News correspondent Jim Acosta stated that "when a child is missing, chances are good it was a convicted sex offender."[41] In actuality, it is far more likely that the child ran away, got lost, or was abducted by a family member.

Radford complains that such distortions make it more difficult to protect children from real dangers. He explains:

> While the abduction, rape, and killing of children by strangers is very, very rare, such incidents receive a lot of media coverage, leading the public to overestimate how common these cases are. Most sexually abused children are not victims of convicted sex offenders [or] Internet pornographers, and most sex offenders do not re-offend once released. This information is rarely mentioned by journalists more interested in sounding alarms than objective analysis. One tragic result of these myths is that the panic over sex offenders distracts the public from a far greater threat to children: parental abuse and neglect.[42]

Fear

Some say that even more than blaming the wrong people, the media intentionally seek to inspire fear among the public, because then the public increasingly turns to the media for further information on the subject. That is, creating fear in citizens increases the power of the media. In a May 2011 article on media distortions, Mike Thomas of the *Orlando Sentinel*—himself a member of the media—complains about this manipulation, saying, "The media have turned the news into a pulp-fiction novel populated with the wildest assortment of crimes, criminals, and characters you could ever imagine. It all is true because what we report did occur to some degree. It also is all a lie because it greatly distorts reality as a whole."[43]

The reality in regard to people who prey on children, Thomas says, is that crime rates are going down and children are being more careful online. Consequently he rejects the idea that countless on-line predators are "trolling for kids," calling such predators nothing more than "bogeymen haunting our waking moments."[44] Thomas adds that people's exposure to news programs has a lot to do with the spread of this kind of fear, quoting criminol-ogist Ted Chiricos as saying, "Seeing local television news seven or more times a week is a fear trigger. People who watch with that kind of frequency are twice as fearful as those who don't watch local news at all."[45]

Others counter that parents' fears about the Internet are justified because the risk of victimization is not zero. Some children do encounter predators or age-inappropri-ate images online, and the consequences of such an en-counter can be devastating. At its website Childwelfare.com, the Child Welfare Research Institute reports:

> While most mature adults are not adversely af-fected by such material, some users—children and youth—are not so immune. There is a considerable body of research that shows that young children are often seri-ously impacted by such material (although, for obvious reasons, there is limited experimental data—children can-not be experimented on as though they were laboratory animals). The clinical research demonstrates that children exposed to pornography will have it show up in dreams and nightmares. This type of material is very confusing and highly emotionally charged for children and can have serious long-term consequences on emotional and ego de-velopment. That's why exposing minors—intentionally or unintentionally—is considered child sexual abuse.[46]

Serious Financial Losses

In regard to financial predation, people tend to argue about a dif-ferent kind of risk. Because it is so difficult to get accurate statistics on how many people have actually encountered a financial preda-tor online, discussions tend to focus on what the most common scams are and just how serious each one can be for victims. At the

"The media have turned the news into a pulp-fiction novel populated with the wildest assortment of crimes, criminals, and characters you could ever imagine."[43]

— Mike Thomas of the *Orlando Sentinel.*

Friends

Experts in online safety advise people to be as careful about revealing their friends' personal information as they are about revealing their own information. As an example of why this is important, the "Internet Safety" section of the website of the Washington State Office of the Attorney General shares a real case involving a girl on a public social networking site who made her profile there anonymous and took great care not to reveal any personal information elsewhere online.

Unfortunately, just three comments from her friends on the site could allow strangers to know exactly who the girl was, where she lived, where she went to school, and how old she was. These comments related to the girl's upcoming birthday party, including where and when it would be held, and an upcoming sporting event that the girl would be attending. Thanks to the photos of the girl that her friends posted, a sexual predator would easily be able to pick her out at these events.

---

forefront of these discussions is the International Mass-Marketing Fraud Working Group (IMMFWG), a group comprised of law enforcement and regulatory and consumer-protection agencies from various countries that conducted an assessment of online financial predation through May 2010.

According to the IMMFWG, "Financial losses do not fully reflect all of the costs that . . . victims often bear. For some victims, the risks extend well beyond loss of personal savings or funds to include physical risks, loss of their homes, depression, and even contemplated, attempted, or actual suicide."[47] In other words, whereas some people consider financial predation less serious than sexual predation because the former is "just" about money, the IMMFWG found that financial predation is as dangerous as sexual predation to victims' emotional and physical well-being.

In supporting this position, the group provided several stories of people who were devastated by financial fraud. These include the case of a British couple in their sixties who suffered severe depression after losing more than $2.7 million to a financial predator. As a result of this loss, the woman attempted suicide twice. Other victims have been physically abused by family members upset over how much money they have lost or by financial predators who have conned them into a face-to-face meeting. In fact, law enforcement agencies have reported that certain financial scams rely on convincing victims to travel to another country, usually Africa, where they will be kidnapped and held for ransom. In one such case in 2008, a group of South African and Nigerian kidnappers demanded a ransom of $5 million for a Japanese businessman who became the victim of an investment scam.

Damaged Trust

In addition to physical dangers, financial loss, and depression, victims of financial fraud suffer a loss of trust from which many say they will never recover. This is particularly the case with romance scam victims, whose involvement with a predator might be extensive. Such victims often send gifts or loans of money out of a desire to help a person with whom they believe they have a close relationship. The predator might make up elaborate stories regarding why the money is needed: to pay a hospital bill, for example, or to pay for a travel visa so the two "lovers" can be together. Victims who feel loved and needed while the scam is taking place typically feel used and abused afterward.

Victims of financial scams perpetrated through bogus online auctions and other financial transactions experience another type of lost trust, the kind that makes it hard for them to put their faith in online merchants. As the IMMFWG notes, a fraud of this nature "has a substantial impact on economies and markets by undermining consumer trust and confidence in legitimate businesses."[48] Thanks in large part to media reports of significant losses due to online theft of credit card information, a 2009 study by the Office of Fair Trading in Great Britain found that a third of

Internet users will not shop online because of distrust and fears of fraud. Another study by security software company AVG found that nearly 90 percent of people in the United Kingdom are more afraid of becoming victims of cybertheft than they are of becoming victims of any other crime. This is akin to the level of panic reached by many parents of teenagers in regard to sexual predators.

The Media's Role

Indeed, psychologists say that media sensationalism regarding crime has in many places produced a phenomenon called the crime complex, whereby public anxiety about crime is the norm. As a result, varying levels of anxiety, panic, or paranoia affect all aspects of people's daily lives, traumatizing even those who have never been victims of a criminal act. Moreover, as the line between what has actually happened and what might happen becomes blurred, people increasingly call for legislation to address problems that do not exist. Such laws might be so restrictive that important personal freedoms would be lost.

Consequently many people criticize the media for spreading fear of online predation. Others, however, note that the media can play an important role in helping victims and reducing preda-

Online auction sites enable just about anyone to sell any item to the highest bidder. While many items posted on auction sites are exactly what they appear to be, some are not. Stories of scams involving fake merchants and fake merchandise create fear among consumers.

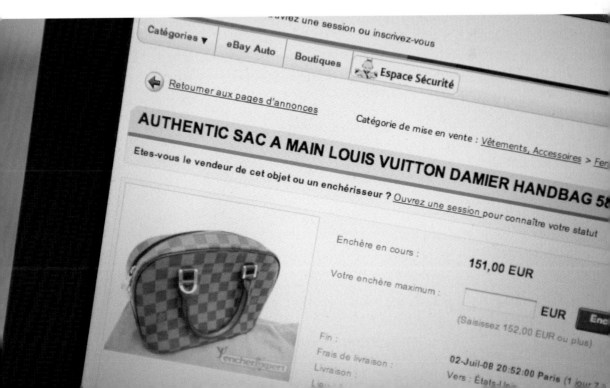

tion. Stories about individuals who have been defrauded because of online activities can serve to educate the public while showing other victims that they are not alone. In addition, media stories that stress the importance of reporting online crimes and provide information on how to make such reports can make it easier for law enforcement agencies to track down predators and reduce the number of victims.

Therefore, cyberpsychologist Kostas Mavropalias says, "The role of the media (television, blogs, online news outlets and more) is critical in the process of educating the public." She argues, however, that the media must adopt "a concise and sensible approach, devoid of fear-mongering and shock practices"[49] in reporting stories related to online predation. Only by taking such an approach, she insists, will people be able to make rational, well-informed decisions about laws and policies proposed to combat predation. Otherwise they might allow unnecessary fears to convince them to give up their privacy and sacrifice online freedoms needlessly, wrongly believing that in exchange they will be making the Internet safer.

Facts

- The CyberTipline of the Exploited Children Division at the National Center for Missing and Exploited Children in Alexandria, Virginia, an international clearinghouse for reports about crimes related to the sexual exploitation of children via the Internet, received nearly 1 million reports between its inception in 1998 and the end of 2010.

- Various studies suggest that no more than 5 percent of crimes related to online sexual predation that result in arrest involve physical violence as opposed to nonviolent means of sexual exploitation.

- Some insurance companies offer identity theft insurance, which covers a certain portion of expenses related to reporting the crime and prosecuting the offender.

- Digital certificates like VeriSign appear on certain websites to indicate that they are secure places to provide financial information; by clicking on the logo of such certificates, users can verify that the site is legitimate rather than a clone of the site set up by a financial predator.

- Studies have found that from 2004 to 2009, the number of young people using the Internet and the number of arrests of online sexual predators rose by roughly the same amount, 20 percent and 21 percent respectively.

Can the Legal System Stop Online Predators?

One of the most recent highly publicized cases associated with online predation involves a pair of suspected serial killers who found their victims on the Internet. Fifty-two-year-old Richard Beasley and 16-year-old Brogan Rafferty are suspected of placing help wanted ads on the Craigslist website in 2011. The ads sought workers for a remote cattle ranch in eastern Ohio. The ranch did not exist; the alleged killers had made it up in order to lure the victims to their death.

First, though, Beasley conducted "job interviews" at an Akron, Ohio, mall. One of the "applicants" who attended an interview there later said that Beasley had told him over 100 people had responded to the ad. So far three deaths have been connected to the "Craigslist killers," as the media have dubbed them, along with one victim who was shot by Rafferty but survived.

A Survivor's Story

This survivor, 48-year-old Scott Davis from South Carolina, escaped the killers after hiding in the woods near a rural road in Noble County, Ohio, for seven hours before going for help. Davis subsequently told police about the ad and the 688-acre cattle ranch (278 ha), then said that two men, one of them Beasley, drove him to a rural area that they said was near the property. The men claimed that a landslide had blocked the road into the ranch and said they would have to walk through heavy woods to get there on foot. Along the way, Davis turned around to talk to his companions, and saw that one of them was pointing a gun at his head. He started running and was shot in the arm while getting away.

One week later, another man was killed in the same area, and police later found a body buried there as well, shot in the head. These two were eventually identified as Ralph Geiger, age 56, and David Pauley, age 51. Another victim, 47-year-old Timothy Kern, was found in a shallow grave near a mall. Kern had last been seen alive November 13, 2011, when he told family members that he had accepted a job he found through Craigslist.

Ohio attorney general Mike DeWine later said there might be even more victims. "We are dealing with serial killings here," he said. "Are there more bodies? Frankly, we don't know. If there are, we need to find them."[50] Both men were awaiting trial for murder. Rafferty's father has said that his son was a victim too. According to Michael Rafferty, his son had been manipulated and possibly abused by Beasley, a longtime family friend who had falsely claimed to be a chaplain concerned with helping the homeless. Indeed, the Craigslist ad targeted older, single, jobless men likely to be homeless in the hope that no one would miss them when they disappeared.

Tracking Down Online Predators

In tracking down the alleged killers and building a case against them, the police used the same methods they would for a murder unassociated with the Internet (although an e-mail did help them identify one of the bodies). This is typically true in other cases where victim and perpetrator come face to face. Such interactions usually create hard evidence that law enforcement officers can use to track down and convict the perpetrator. In addition, as with the Craigslist killer case, there are often witnesses whose recollections can help police capture the perpetrator.

Restricting Internet Access

The common perception is that regardless of having received therapy, sex offenders are highly likely to repeat their crimes. This is why legislators have enacted strict laws that prevent released sex offenders from living near a school or engaging in activities that would put them into close contact with children. In 2011 the state of Louisiana created a law that would also prevent registered sex offenders from using social networking sites and chat rooms. However, the American Civil Liberties Union filed a complaint in federal court to block the law, contending that it violates the offenders' constitutional right to free speech and equal treatment as US citizens. In addition, others have argued that people are needlessly panicking about the likelihood of an online sexual predator reoffending, since according to the US Justice Department, sex offenders are 25 percent less likely to be rearrested than all other criminals. But those who want to restrict Internet use by sexual predators say that these low rates are due to the strict laws already in place and can be made still lower by even tougher laws.

In Internet-connected cases where anonymity is not breached, however, it is more difficult for law enforcement officers to identify the perpetrator and gather enough evidence to make an arrest and gain a conviction. Consequently they often resort to ruses designed to draw predators out into the open. Had police used this approach to find the Craigslist killers, for example, they would have answered the ad pretending to be a job applicant in order to meet with the killers in person.

One of the most common ruses related to online crime is designed to catch sexual predators. This ruse, typically known as a sting operation, uses undercover officers posing as kids on the Internet in order to trick potential offenders into meeting in person. These officers participate in teen chat rooms and other sites online where predators tend to hunt for victims, engaging possible predators in conversations designed to elicit offers to meet in person. When a predator shows up at a prearranged meeting place, he finds law enforcement officers there to arrest him.

One such sting operation in Kentucky, for example, made sexual predators think that they were chatting online with a 12-year-old girl over a period of anywhere from one day to several weeks. Over the course of these conversations, the perpetrators described in detail the sexual acts they planned to perform with the girl. Some also sent her pornographic images. The adult pretending to be the girl never initiated the sending of these images or the sexually explicit conversations; instead, it was left to the perpetrator to bring up such topics. In one case, it took only 12 minutes for the perpetrator to start talking about sex. Ultimately seven of the predators were conned into showing up at a particular house where they thought they would be having sex with the girl. All were arrested for soliciting sex with a minor.

"Law enforcement officers have learned that it is relatively easy to lure people into committing a sexual crime, and that sexual cases are politically popular to prosecute and very unpopular to defend."[52]

— Defense attorney Thomas A. Pavlinic.

Television Involvement

In creating this sting operation, which took place in 2006, Kentucky law enforcement partnered with a group called Perverted-Justice, whose members played the part of the underage girl. Perverted-Justice also partnered with law enforcement as part of a TV series produced by the TV newsmagazine program *Dateline NBC* that made such undercover antipredator efforts famous: *To Catch a Predator*, which ran from November 2004 to December 2007. In all, *To Catch a Predator* worked on 12 investigations across the United States, using hidden cameras to show the predator's reaction to discovering that the house he had entered held not an underage girl but the host of the show, Chris Hansen. When Hansen then questioned the predators about their intentions, most of them insisted they went to the house thinking they would be having sex with an adult, even though transcripts of the related online conversations show that the girl clearly identified herself as a minor.

With the first two *To Catch a Predator* investigations, no law enforcement officers were on-site, so the ensnared men were allowed to leave the house without being arrested. In subsequent investigations, officers were present to take predators away. However, in one 2006 case officers allowed the suspect—a Texas assistant district attorney named Louis Conradt—to leave the filming location. He then went home and fatally shot himself just as a SWAT team was trying to serve him with a search warrant.

Entrapment

This death led many people to criticize the show for unduly humiliating people who had not yet been proven guilty of any crime. The same criticisms arose in Germany in 2010 regarding a TV program inspired by *To Catch a Predator*, because an alleged child abuser disappeared after leaving the house where he was lured. He has not been found, and his family fears he is dead. Those associat-

Sheriff's deputies escort Brogan Rafferty to the courthouse in 2011. Rafferty is one of two people accused of robbing and killing job seekers responding to fake help wanted ads placed on Craigslist.

ed with the German show say they cannot understand why people are so worried about a suspected pedophile, but the justice minister, Sabine Leutheusser-Schnarrenberger, counters that it is wrong to publicly accuse someone of pedophilia without giving them the chance to defend themselves first. "There is the danger [with such TV shows] that innocents will be put in the stocks and damage caused, and the rule of law will be thrown out of balance."[51]

These shows have also led to criticisms regarding the techniques that law enforcement officers use to draw predators out into the open. Some say these techniques border on or are entrapment, the act of inducing a person to commit a crime that he or she would not otherwise be predisposed to commit. In the United States, entrapment is illegal, so people who can prove they were entrapped must be set free. In the case of *To Catch a Predator*, Perverted-Justice and producers insisted that perpetrators were always the first ones to bring up discussions of sex, which would mean that no entrapment took place. Others involved with the show, however, have said that this was not necessarily the case, and sometimes the method of tricking the predator was so unclear that officials refused to prosecute someone snared by the show.

Widespread Use

Nonetheless, such efforts to lure potential predators to their arrest is the primary way that law enforcement agencies try to combat online sexual predation. The main reason this approach is so prominent is due to government funding. In 1998, because of growing fears of online sexual predation, the US Congress funded the creation of the Internet Crimes Against Children task force, which immediately began providing federal grants to local law enforcement agencies that wanted to launch online sting operations. As a result, federal and state authorities have devoted more effort to catching sexual predators. According to defense attorney Thomas A. Pavlinic, however, money is not the only reason for these efforts. He says, "Law enforcement officers have learned that it is relatively easy to lure people into committing a sexual crime, and that sexual cases are politically popular to prosecute and very unpopular to defend."[52] Pavlinic's law firm, the Premier Defense

Group, specializes in defending such cases, which it says are often the result of people being unfairly swept up in sting operations.

Despite the efforts of such law firms, online sting operations tend to have a high success rate. For example, in a December 2009 *Vanity Fair* article, journalist Mark Bowden reports on a Pennsylvania operation with a nearly 100 percent conviction rate. However, Bowden also casts doubt on whether everyone who is convicted is 100 percent guilty.

Specifically, Bowden describes a case involving a man he calls only "J." In an online chat room, J encountered a woman called Deery seeking adult males who would pay to have sex with under-

Wiring Money

An American company that electronically transfers funds instantaneously from one bank account to another for a fee, Western Union is often used as a tool to commit online financial fraud. This is especially true when the scammer is outside the United States. To try to combat this problem, Western Union warns all customers not to send money to anyone they have never met in person. However, people succumbing to advance-fee scams, romance scams, and similar forms of financial fraud rarely heed the warning. Western Union also maintains records regarding each transaction, showing who sent the money and to whom it was sent, but they will not release this information without a court order, and in any case the scammers usually use fake names and IDs. Moreover, the receiver of the money can pick it up anywhere in the world. Consequently it is difficult for victims to recover money wired overseas. As a result, some websites that handle financial transactions, including the online auction site e-bay, ban the use of Western Union wire transfers as a form of payment.

age girls she claimed were her daughters. This woman was actually a police officer, and whenever a man would agree to meet with her and her daughters, authorities would consider this as proof that the man was willing to commit a sexual offense. Consequently the man would arrive at the meeting to find a team of armed police officers waiting for him.

J talked with this woman for several days before agreeing to get together with her and her daughters, and even then he said that he wanted to meet with the woman first alone. Later, after he was arrested, he said it was because he never intended to meet with the girls at all. He was only interested in the woman, he insisted. He also insisted that when he was talking with Deery about having sex with her daughters, he was simply expressing a fantasy, not stating an intention. "I certainly had no intention of [having sex with the daughters]," J told Bowden. "I intended to have sex with [the mother] and then leave. Period."[53] Nonetheless, according to Bowden, the police took the position that once a person began making arrangements for an actual, face-to-face meeting, the Internet conversation left the fantasy world and entered the real world.

Pitfalls and Advantages of Stings

This case illustrates the main problem with online predator sting operations: How do prosecutors prove without doubt that the alleged predator would actually have gone through with the crime? Is it not possible that a potential predator, finally seeing his potential victim in person, might suddenly decide not to engage in any sexual acts? Internet sting operations aimed at predators typically do not allow for this change of heart.

Therefore, Bowden points out, people might be imprisoned for only a thought rather than a deed, an approach that could lead to abuses. This kind of operation, he says, "leads unavoidably into the gray area of thoughts, intentions, and predispositions—and into the equally murky realm of enticement and entrapment. It is a way of conducting police business that, without extreme care, can itself become a form of abuse—in which the pursuer and the pursued grow entangled in a transaction that takes on a gruesome life of its own."[54]

Even so, many law enforcement officers, prosecutors, and others involved with anticrime efforts argue that online sting operations are the best and usually the only way to address sexual predation connected to Internet use. For example, Ted Belling of Case Law 4 Cops, which provides police officers with information on how to avoid engaging in entrapment, says there are only two ways to catch an online predator: one that depends on a victim, and one without a victim. The first way begins with the victim coming forward to reveal that a sexual offense has taken place. Usually what follows is a lot of difficult police work that might or might not result in tracking down, arresting, and prosecuting the suspect—if the victim is willing and able to endure being a witness in a court trial. The second way is an online sting whereby the only people involved, besides the predator, are law enforcement authorities who know how to achieve an arrest and gain the conviction of the predator. About this second option Belling says, "The online sting is the most effective way to hunt and capture predators while eliminating the trauma suffered on a young victim. I am sure every officer would agree that catching the predator before he actually harms a child is much better than waiting until he sexually abuses the child."[55]

> "The online sting is the most effective way to hunt and capture predators while eliminating the trauma suffered on a young victim."[55]
>
> — Ted Belling of Case Law 4 Cops.

Sentencing Problems

Once predators are identified, however, it is not always easy to punish them enough to satisfy society. For example, "J" served only a year in prison, which many would say is not nearly enough time if he was truly guilty of planning to sexually assault two underage girls. Similarly, in 2011, 22-year-old Jesus Felix of Los Angeles, California, was punished with just 30 days of road-crew service after he created 130 fake Facebook pages, as well as listings on the Craigslist website, in order to share personal information and photos that devastated his 16-year-old ex-girlfriend. However, he was also required to attend therapy sessions and anger-management classes.

Felix was arrested and charged under a 2011 California law making it a misdemeanor crime to impersonate someone else, real or fake, on the Internet for malicious purposes. This law arose because of the public outcry that occurred when a woman was deemed not guilty of any crime for pretending to be a teenage boy so she could harass a 13-year-old girl on MySpace. The victim, targeted because the woman's daughter did not like her, ultimately committed suicide because of the harassment. Police only learned the identity of the harasser, dubbed "the MySpace Mom," because of an informant. Under the new law, the woman would have received up to a year in jail and a $1,000 fine for impersonating a teenager.

Many people say this is still not enough. But at least it is more than in most states, which fail to legally address the issue at all. Nearly all cases of malicious Internet impersonation go unpunished. In addition, a 2009 Texas law similar to the California law, making it either a misdemeanor or a felony (depending on the

A police officer in Georgia logs into a chat room as part of her department's efforts to crack down on online sexual predators. Officers sometimes try to flush out potential predators by posing as teenagers online.

severity of the offense) to impersonate others on social networking sites, is being challenged as violating people's right to free speech. This constitutional issue is preventing many other laws from being enacted to deal with Internet anonymity and the type of conversations and images that appear online. In fact, shortly before the 2011 California law was enacted, critics said it could have a chilling effect on free speech and might even be used to suppress political speech.

Financial Fraud Challenges

IMMFWG reports that fraud efforts are becoming increasingly cooperative, with groups changing associates depending on the needs of a particular scam. The IMMFWG also says that financial predators who market their scams to large numbers of people are "highly adaptive, rapidly changing their methods and techniques to reduce the risks of law enforcement detection and investigation and to respond to consumer and business awareness of their current methods."[56] Many of these mass-market scams are based in countries such as Nigeria that provide relatively safe havens for predators.

To address such challenges, the IMMFWG argues, investigative, law enforcement, and regulatory authorities in multiple countries must coordinate their efforts so they can expand their ability to gather intelligence, share information and resources, and disrupt crime operations. They must also work together to enforce laws related to predation, prosecute offenders, and help those who have been victimized. In addition, the IMMFWG says, authorities must devote more effort and resources to public awareness and education programs directed at both individuals and businesses. This group and many others emphasize the importance of education because they believe it is far easier to prevent predation than to capture and convict predators.

Facts

- According to the National Center for Missing and Exploited Children, as of March 2011 there were 728,435 registered sex offenders in the United States, but law enforcement authorities were unable to account for the whereabouts of roughly 100,000 of them.

- Computer forensics is a branch of digital science that involves retrieving legal evidence from computers and other digital storage media.

- A common type of Internet fraud relies on fake ads for security software to trick people into paying to remove malicious software, or malware, from their computers, when in fact the payment results in malware being added to the computer.

- In February 2011 the US government launched Operation Save Our Children to combat child pornography on the Internet, but while shutting down illegal websites that distributed this pornography it also accidentally shut down over 84,000 legal, non-pornographic sites.

- According to the Perverted-Justice website, between June 2004 and October 2011, 548 predators were convicted because of the group's online predator sting operations.

CHAPTER FIVE

Can Prevention Efforts Protect Online Users from Predators?

I n March 2011 Canadian police staff sergeant Darren Laur of Victoria, British Columbia, spoke to teenagers at a school about Internet safety. He talked about the importance of not befriending strangers online, stressing that one never knows whether a stranger is telling the truth about who he or she is. Many members of his audience nodded in agreement. Then he revealed that 30 of the students had allowed Laur access to their Facebook accounts, thinking he was a 15-year-old girl they had never met. One of the boys in the audience had even asked Laur's false persona for a date.

Demonstrations of Vulnerability

The students were stunned by this information. They never imagined that the Facebook account they thought belonged to a 15-year-old girl was actually a fake created by a 46-year-old man. Several were also upset to realize that they had voluntarily given that man, Laur, their phone numbers and descriptions of their homes, school, and family members. Some had also provided details about their schedules and the routines of those they lived with. Laur told the students that using this information and cell-phone technology, he could determine the location of their house and know when they would be there alone.

Suzanne Stanford's teenage daughter had a similar wake-up call several years ago, when her mother showed her how vulnerable she was to online predation. An Internet safety expert in Southern California, Stanford had been planning to make a presentation concerning safety issues related to MySpace when she decided to see just how much information its teen users were sharing there. She explains: "Since I wasn't too familiar, I signed up for Myspace .com and I pretended to be a 15-year-old kid that lived in the Newport [California] area. I just put in there that I'm a 15-year-old kid and I'm interested in drama and singing and things my daughter was interested in. Then I started looking for friends, and much to my surprise, I found my daughter."[57]

On the site, Stanford's daughter had posted her picture along with her last name and home city. Using this information, Stanford was able to find the house address online, and by using the website Google Earth she was able to view a photograph of the house. In fact, Google's zoom feature allowed her to view the place as though she were standing at the edge of its driveway. When Stanford showed her daughter what she had discovered, the girl was horrified. "She almost fell off her chair," Stanford reports. "I said, 'What if I was a bad guy? All I would have to do is lie in wait for you.' That's how easy it is."[58]

Some law enforcement officers involved in teen Internet safety education take this lesson a step further. After searching online for a teen who shares enough information to be located offline, the officer will confront the teen at home, school, or afterschool hangouts in order to shock him or her into recognizing that it is dangerous to share identifying information online. For example, an undercover officer in Australia was able to track down a girl named Shannon after she told him the name of her school, the name of her afterschool basketball team, and her player number, 7.

After the girl, who thought she was talking to a 14-year-old boy online, revealed that she played basketball every Thursday afternoon, the officer went to the court on a Thursday, watched the basketball game, and then followed player number 7 home. As

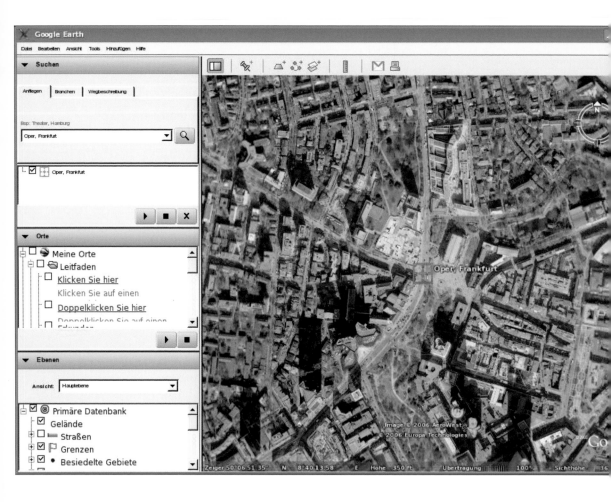

A California Internet safety expert vividly demonstrated the potential danger of putting personal information on social networking sites. Using Google Earth (a screen shot appears here) and information on her teenage daughter's MySpace page, the woman was able to precisely locate their house.

he walked behind her, he saw that her name was printed on the back of her shirt, confirming that he had the right "victim." Soon he was at her house, telling her father who he was and how he had found a now horrified Shannon.

An Unnecessary Lesson

Such demonstrations of vulnerability are often successful. Someone from the British Columbia Ministry of Education who attended one of Laur's demonstrations, for example, later expressed confidence that most of the teens in the audience would change their behavior because of their experience, and Stanford's daughter removed her personal information from MySpace. Nonetheless, some people argue that these demonstrations are pointless because teens do not need to worry about strangers tracking them down.

For example, in a survey of law enforcement agencies dealing with online sexual predation, researchers with the University of New Hampshire specifically asked whether officers had encountered a predator who found victims in this way. They failed to come across any cases where a predator had used information posted online to find, stalk, and possibly abduct unsuspecting victims. Moreover, the researchers uncovered only three cases where offline stalking occurred, but in every case, the victim had already met face-to-face with the predator before the stalking began. However, the researchers also said that none of these stalking cases involved violence and probably would not have been considered serious enough, from a legal standpoint, for police to arrest the stalker.

Temporary Success

Other people argue that demonstrations like Laur's are unnecessary because they will not change teens' online behavior in the long run. That is, young people might think twice about sharing personal information in the weeks right after a wake-up call, but as time passes they will probably grow careless again. This idea is supported by a study conducted by a federal online safety task force. In 2010 the Online Safety and Technology Working Group (OSTWG), created by the National Telecommunications and Information Administration, reported that students who spend a large amount of time on social networking sites or using text messaging or similar ways to communicate are not influenced by scare tactics related to Internet safety.

One reason that scare tactics can be ineffective is their reliance on exaggerations and other distortions related to risk assessment. When a teenager realizes that one part of a discussion is a lie, he or she will dismiss any of the accurate information provided at the same time. As an example of a common exaggeration related to predation that can "turn off" listeners, the OSTWG cited cases where teens are told that there is a high risk they will be physically assaulted by an online stranger when in fact "the statistical probability of a young

> *"The statistical probability of a young person being physically assaulted by an adult who they first met online is extremely low."* [59]
>
> — Online Safety and Technology Working Group.

Chat Room Safety Tips

Although many Internet safety experts believe that young people should not use online chat rooms, they do offer tips to those who do visit such places. First, they recommend the use of monitored chat rooms only, where reputable adults supervise all conversations. Second, they advise young people never to reveal any personal information in a chat room, even to the point of using a gender-neutral nickname so predators cannot tell whether they are dealing with a girl or a boy. Third, they warn users to watch out for leading questions, which are questions that seem harmless but are designed to gradually draw out sensitive information; anyone who is asking too many questions should be avoided. Fourth, they tell users to ignore all invitations to take their public conversation to a private chat room or into private messaging. And finally, they ask young people to report to their parents any comment that makes them uncomfortable.

person being physically assaulted by an adult who they first met online is extremely low."[59]

Another reason scare tactics do not work on teens is that people of this age are rarely frightened by statistics. Parenting expert Denise Witmer, whose background is in child and social psychology, explains, "Developmentally, teens are still getting the gist of reality. The thought that 'something could happen' means to a teen that 'something will happen to someone else, but not me.'"[60]

Nonetheless, Internet safety experts stress the importance of trying to impress upon kids the fact that the online world is more like a public bulletin board than a private notebook. Frederick S. Lane argues: "It's unrealistic . . . to keep our children off the Internet altogether, and it's counterproductive to raise them in a fog of fear, but it's a valuable exercise to make them think about what information they're sharing, who has access to it, and what the consequences could be if it reaches a larger-than-intended audience."[61]

Even a reasonable, well-informed discussion with teens about Internet risks might not affect their online behavior, however. This is because, given enough time in a conversation, most people will naturally start talking about the things they have, the places they have been, and the kind of life they live. Consequently, spending a significant amount of time online without sharing personal information is hard to do.

Not surprisingly, in 2010 the Internet security company McAfee, Inc., reported that its study of teen behavior on the Internet found that despite widespread warnings about online dangers, nearly 70 percent of teens continue to share their physical location on social networking sites, and nearly a third continue to talk to strangers online, often providing their first name while doing so. Tracy Mooney of McAfee says, "Kids know not to talk to strangers—it's one of the first lessons you teach them. But online, there's a sense of trust and anonymity, so kids let their guard down. Kids would never hand out their name and address to a stranger in the real world, so it's alarming to see how many kids do that very thing online."[62]

> "The thought that 'something could happen' means to a teen that 'something will happen to someone else, but not me.'"[60]
>
> — Parenting expert Denise Witmer.

Parental Monitoring

The McAfee study also indicates, however, that parental monitoring can be successful in reducing the kind of online behavior that leads teens into trouble. Over a third of teens say they do not want their parents to know what they are doing online and would change their Internet behavior if they knew their parents were watching them. Consequently, Mooney advises parents to be highly involved in the decisions their kids make online.

Sometimes this involvement is easy for parents to accomplish. For example, Michele Graham, a mother of two children in Newport, California, says, "A rule in our house has always been no chat rooms. We have one computer, and it's in our family room, so whenever you're on the computer, there's always an adult in the room."[63] Sometimes, however, parental involvement takes some work. For example, Lane monitors his kids' Facebook pages regularly in order to make sure they are not communicating with the wrong people or in inappropriate ways. Lane says: "There was one brief period when my older son tinkered with his privacy settings and 'forgot' to include me in his inner circle, but when asked about it, he quickly restored the default. There's no question that kids (including my own) express annoyance about this level of supervision, but, in the long run, I believe it comforts them to know that someone is looking out for them and cares about what they're doing online."[64]

Monitoring a teen's activities can cause inconveniences to the teen as well. For example, Michael Miller, a reporter who interviewed parents about their Internet safety practices, says: "The Internet may harbor dangers, but it also harbors major resources for any student, which makes supervision difficult at times." For example, one of the mothers said her daughter "was sometimes unable to do biology research online because she and her husband had blocked certain websites."[65]

Filtering Software

In bringing up blocked websites, Miller was referring to Internet filtering software that prevents various websites from being accessed by young people, and may monitor their visits to unblocked sites as well. Filtering software can also limit people's exposure to unsolicited advertisements, whether on websites or via e-mail. Such filters do reduce users' contact with potential predators. However, no software can prevent all contact with predators. Consequently, many Internet security experts advise parents not to rely entirely on tools to protect their teens. Instead, parents should take responsibility for knowing what their teens are doing online and for creating an environment where teens feel safe enough to share any concerns about their online experiences.

Nonetheless, some US laws have placed part of this responsibility with schools. For example, the Children's Internet Protection Act (CIPA), signed into law in 2000, requires libraries and schools that receive federal funding and are attended by students in kindergarten through grade 12 to implement an Internet safety policy. This policy not only blocks minors' access to inappropriate material on the Internet but also monitors the online activities of minors, ensuring their safety when they are using e-mail, chat rooms, and other forms of electronic communication. The 2008 Protecting Children in the 21st Century Act also requires schools to teach students about Internet safety. In part because of such laws, a 2011 study by the Pew Internet & American Life Project found that 70 percent of teens report having received online safety advice from a teacher or other adult at school. Eighty-six percent also received such advice from parents, while 54 percent received it from the media.

Romantic Notions

Educational programs typically focus on preventing people from unintentionally becoming a victim of an online predator. This means the programs usually fail to address situations in which an individual intentionally seeks out someone whom he or she believes to be a decent person but who turns out to be a predator. This is often true with victims of financial fraud, many of whom are scammed after willingly entering into online transactions with people they believe to be honest. It is also the case with teenagers who interact with a predator under the mistaken notion that they are involved in a romantic relationship. Such cases suggest that prevention efforts should focus on psychology rather than technology, exploring the reasons why someone feels the need to approach and trust an online stranger.

This approach to prevention would have to include discussions that make sure teens are getting the right messages regarding sex. The University of New Hampshire researchers have concluded that "more efforts need to be made to educate and discourage teens from engaging in sexual and romantic relationships with older partners."[66] They add that young people need to be given information about laws regarding age of consent so they know what constitutes rape, and they need to understand the emotional consequences of a minor engaging in sexual conversations with adults or having consensual sex with an adult. An approach that seeks to address teenagers' false notions about sex and romance, the researchers say, is "more likely to address the real dynamics of the crime [of sexual predation] than warnings about being stalked by someone who obtains personal information posted online."[67]

Types of Risk

Experts currently researching online predation classify intentional behavior that leads to an encounter with a predator as a conduct risk. Such risks occur specifically because of the way an individual

Permanent and Not Always Private

Many Internet security experts say that one of the problems with keeping teens safe online is that this age group has trouble with the concept that information shared online is difficult if not impossible to delete. That is, teens do not generally understand the permanence of their actions. Many also do not know that deleting something from the Internet does not necessarily mean it is gone. Certain websites can save information and images without users' knowledge, and even seemingly fleeting conversations can still be stored in cyberspace. For example, in 2010, EchoMetrix, a New York-based company that markets software to parents who want a record of their teens' online instant messaging conversations, admitted to sharing these conversations—without the knowledge of the parents or the teens—with companies interested in finding out what people were saying about their products and services. (The company was subsequently fined by the state of New York for doing this and banned from continuing the practice.) There have also been cases where employees at social networking sites like Facebook, which stores messages in a database even after they have been deleted, have accessed users' private information without authorization.

conducts himself or herself online. A contact risk is an action that might lead to accidental contact with a predator. A content risk might expose someone to an unwanted, inappropriate image or website. A 2011 report by the Family Online Safety Institute (FOSI), which has studied online predation throughout the world, says that all three types of risk must be addressed in prevention efforts.

In addition, the report argues, all people connected to the problem of online predation must work together to solve it: parents, teachers, law enforcement, government, Internet safety organizations, and the Internet industry. Young people must also be empowered with ways to keep themselves safe while online. Moreover, FOSI argues, combating predation should be a global effort, with well-developed countries working to educate parents in developing countries so that their young people can be protected as well. FOSI reports that "the way children use technology and the risks they face are remarkably similar around the world. Often the biggest variable is the way adult society in a given country deals with the risks and actual harm."[68]

FOSI further reports that inaccurate perceptions related to risk are a global problem. Their report explains:

> Adult perceptions of risk sometimes bear little relationship to the actual risks, and resulting government initiatives are often slow to prevent actual harm. Major variation exists in what aspects of online risk countries focus on and how they decide to build legislation and programs to cope with them. The digital development of countries plays a large part in determining how online safety is handled in both legislation and education.[69]

Struggling with Anonymity

In other words, all countries struggle to come up with legal and preventive approaches to addressing online predation. Some countries also struggle with the issue of Internet anonymity, try-

"Kids would never hand out their name and address to a stranger in the real world, so it's alarming to see how many kids do that very thing online."[62]

— Tracy Mooney of McAfee, Inc.

ing to determine whether the greater good demands that people attach their real names to the comments and images they share online. Doing so, notes Internet expert Sarah Perez, would make it impossible for users to create false identities "so they can troll around harassing others" and would force them to adhere to "the same standards for behavior that you would expect to see if you encountered them in a real-life public situation."[70]

The end of anonymity would also make it easier for law enforcement to address Internet crime, and this would be especially helpful in combating financial predation because victim and perpetrator so rarely meet face to face. However, civil rights experts warn that ending online anonymity could also give police too much power to violate the rights to privacy and free speech. It might also prevent people from reporting crimes, because criminals would know who reported them. Anonymity, some argue, creates benefits to society that should not be tossed away. The Electronic Privacy Information Center, which supports legal efforts to maintain Internet anonymity, explains that anonymity "allows the persecuted, the underserved, and the simply embarrassed to seek information—and disseminate it—while maintaining their privacy and reputations in both cyberspace and the material world."[71]

Giving Up Freedoms

But before deciding whether it is necessary to give up freedoms, it is important to have a clear view of the seriousness of the Internet predator problem—a view that has not been affected by media sensationalism or law enforcement bias. In regard to the latter, Nancy Willard of the Center for Safe and Responsible Internet Use says that because law enforcement officials have to deal with distraught victims, some of whom have been victimized in horrible ways, "it is not surprising that they approach Internet safety from the perspective of criminal danger."[72] This perspective, she suggests, prevents them from addressing the problem of Internet predation objectively.

The media is not objective either. As media critic Steve Rendall notes, "There is money to be made from fear—and business

Computers at the Boston Public Library (pictured) and other libraries around the country are heavily used. Schools and libraries that receive federal funds must install blocking devices on their computers to prevent patrons from accessing inappropriate material online.

has been good for those hawking the online predator threat."[73] He points out that sensationalized stories about predators sell newspapers and magazines and bring large audiences to TV shows like *To Catch a Predator*. Companies that sell Internet safety software also benefit from predator scares.

However, some businesses lose money because of financial predation, and these have an incentive to launch education programs designed to prevent the problem. As Chief Executive John Fingleton of Britain's Office of Fair Trading says, "Online retailing is the future for many businesses and increasingly important to the economy. If consumers are not confident online, demand will grow at a slower rate. So we must tackle these concerns right now if the online market is to grow at its full potential."[74] Similarly, Facebook, MySpace, and other social networking sites have a motive to keep online predators from ruining their reputations, and, like online retailers, the owners of these sites have worked to educate the public about the dangers of online predation. They have also engaged in such practices as blocking objectionable content and restricting users, in an attempt to limit the way people use their sites.

But Willard suggests that only academics trained to deal objectively with predation issues should be charged with educating people about Internet dangers. She argues, "As we move forward, it is essential that instruction about these concerns be grounded in accurate research and incorporate effective risk prevention approaches targeted at appropriate audiences. Educators with expertise in adolescent development and youth risk prevention—generally the health teachers and guidance counselors—must play a predominant role in addressing these issues with students."[75]

She and many others note that using the Internet clearly has its risks and that sometimes these risks can lead to serious harm. But this is true in regard to certain offline activities as well, and Internet use should not engender any more panic and paranoia that those other activities do. What is needed instead is the kind of awareness that empowers people to avoid victimhood—an awareness that comes from understanding the true nature of the Internet's risks and learning effective strategies to stay away from and/or deal with risky situations.

Facts

- According to the National Center for Missing and Exploited Children, only one-third of US households have Internet filtering or blocking software.

- According to the 2010 *Norton Online Family Report*, six out of ten parents in the United States and Canada say that parents should have total control over what their children do online.

- According to a 2011 study by the Internet security company McAfee, Inc., although many teens have been told that sharing personal information online can jeopardize their safety, 69 percent of those aged 13 to 17 have provided their physical location on social networking sites.

- According to a 2011 survey sponsored by the National Cyber Security Alliance, 80 percent of small businesses in the United States think their computer systems are safe from cyberthieves, which might be why 40 percent reported having no plan in place regarding how to respond to an online security breach that puts customers' credit card information at risk.

- Video chats, which allow users to see and hear the people they are talking to on their computer, can protect users from being tricked by predators adopting false personas—but such chats can also make it easier for predators to victimize users via the unwanted sharing of sexual images.

Related Organizations and Websites

Berkman Center for Internet & Society

Harvard University
23 Everett St., 2nd Floor
Cambridge, MA 02138
phone: (617) 495-7547
e-mail: cyber@law.harvard.edu
website: http://cyber.law.harvard.edu

Founded in 1997, the Berkman Center for Internet & Society conducts research on a variety of issues related to the Internet, including online privacy. Its website includes the 2010 report *Youth, Privacy, and Reputation.*

Center for Safe and Responsible Internet Use (CSRIU)

474 W. Twenty-Ninth Ave.
Eugene, OR 97405
phone: (541) 556-1145
e-mail: contact@csriu.org
website: www.cyberbully.org

Established by Internet safety expert Nancy Willard, the CSRIU offers reports and guides that address issues arising from the use of the Internet in schools.

Chatdanger

website: www.chatdanger.com

The Chatdanger website provides information on the potential dangers of interacting with strangers online, whether in chat rooms or via instant messenger, e-mail, or online games. The site also offers young people a place to share stories or advice related to their online experiences.

ConnectSafely

website: www.connectsafely.org

The ConnectSafely website offers advice for both children and adults on how to practice safe blogging and safe social networking. It offers safety advice, resources related to online safety, and a forum where users can discuss issues related to blogging and networking.

Crimes Against Children Research Center (CRCC)

University of New Hampshire
126 Horton Social Science Center
Durham, NH 03824
phone: (603) 862-1888
e-mail: kelly.foster@unh.edu
website: www.unh.edu

The CCRC works to promote knowledge about and improve strategies for preventing crimes against children. It also helps victims and families cope with the aftermath of crime.

The Family Online Safety Institute (FOSI)

400 Seventh St. NW, Suite 306
Washington, DC 20004
website: www.fosi.org

An international nonprofit organization, FOSI partners with major communications- and entertainment-related companies to develop a safer Internet while still respecting free speech. It also works with Internet safety advocates and others to develop new technology, shape public policy, and promote education related to online safety.

GetNetWise (GNW)

e-mail: cmatsuda@neted.org
website: www.getnetwise.org

GNW is a public service coalition provided by Internet industry corporations and public interest organizations to help ensure that Internet users have safe online experiences. The website offers articles on online child safety, Internet privacy, online social networking, and issues related to financial predation.

Internet Society (ISOC)

1775 Wiehle Ave., Suite 201
Reston, VA 20190-5108
phone: (703) 439-2120
fax: (703) 326-9881
e-mail: isoc@isoc.org
website: ww.isoc.org

The ISOC is an international, nonprofit group founded in 1992 to provide leadership in the formation of Internet-related standards, education, and public policy. Its goal is to ensure the open development of the Internet for the benefit of people throughout the world. The ISOC acts as a global clearinghouse for Internet information and educational materials.

Microsoft Safety and Security Center (MSSC)

website: www.microsoft.com

The MSSC website offers a wealth of information related to computer security, digital privacy, and online safety. It also offers some free downloads of security tools and provides tips on how to create passwords that financial predators will find difficult to guess.

Safe Kids

e-mail: larry@larrymagid.com
website: www.safekids.com

Created in 1994 by technology journalist Larry Magid, SafeKids
.com is one of the oldest websites to provide information on how
children can be safe online. Magid is the author of one of the
earliest brochures on children's online safety, *Child Safety on the
Information Highway*, published in 1994.

Safe Teens

e-mail: larry@larrymagid.com
website: www.safeteens.com

Operated by technology journalist Larry Magid, SafeTeens.com
provides information for teens about how to use the Internet safe-
ly and responsibly. Magid is one of the most prominent critics of
the way the media reports on online safety, arguing that far too
often the risks and dangers of using the Internet are exaggerated.

US Department of Justice

Computer Crimes & Intellectual Property Section (CCIPS)
Tenth and Constitution Ave. NW
Criminal Division
John C. Keeney Bldg., Suite 600
Washington, DC 20530
phone: (202) 514-1026
website: www.cybercrime.gov

Part of the US Department of Justice, the CCIPS implements US
government strategies for combating computer and intellectual
property crimes worldwide and works with other government agencies, the private sector, academic institutions, and foreign counter-
parts to prevent, investigate, and prosecute computer crimes.

Web Wise Kids (WWK)

website: www.webwisekids.org

Founded in 2000 and currently part of the US federal government's Project Safe Childhood initiative, WWK is a national nonprofit organization dedicated to empowering young people to make wise choices online. Its programs help children deal with issues such as sexting, cyberbullying, Internet fraud, and online sexual predation.

Wired Safety

website: www.wiredsafety.org

Founded in 1995, the nonprofit group Wired Safety helps victims of cybercrime and online harassment, assists law enforcement worldwide in preventing and investigating cybercrimes, and disseminates information designed to educate people on privacy, security, and other aspects of online safety.

Additional Reading

Books

Mark Bauerlein, *The Digital Divide: Arguments for and Against Facebook, Google, Texting, and the Age of Social Networking.* New York: Tarcher, 2011.

Richard Guerry, *Public and Permanent: The Golden Rule of the 21st Century.* Bloomington, IN: Balboa, 2011.

Todd Kelsey, *Social Networking Spaces: From Facebook to Twitter and Everything in Between.* New York: Apress, 2010.

Frederick S. Lane, *Cybertraps for the Young.* Chicago: NTI Upstream, 2011.

David A. Montague, *Essentials of Online Payment Security and Fraud Prevention.* New York: John Wiley & Sons, 2010.

John Palfrey, *Born Digital: Understanding the First Generation of Digital Natives.* New York: Basic Books, 2010.

Jeffrey Robinson, *There's a Sucker Born Every Minute: A Revelation of Audacious Frauds, Scams, and Cons—How to Spot Them, How to Stop Them.* New York: Perigee Trade, 2010.

Joseph T. Wells, ed., *Internet Fraud Casebook: The World Wide Web of Deceit.* New York: John Wiley & Sons, 2010.

Periodicals

Greg Ferenstein, "Three Ways Educators Are Embracing Social Technology," *Mashable*, January 10, 2010. http://mashable.com.

Dan Fletcher, "How Facebook Is Redefining Privacy," *Time*, May 20, 2010.

Guilbert Gates, "Facebook Privacy: A Bewildering Tangle of Options," *New York Times*, May 12, 2010.

Sarah Kessler, "The Case for Social Media in Schools," *Mashable*, September 29, 2010. http://mashable.com.

Michael Robertson, "Is Privacy History?," *San Diego Union-Tribune*, November 13, 2011.

Zachary Romano, "Why We Love Social Networking," *Post Standard*, March 1, 2010.

John Timpane, "Tweeting, Blogging and E-Mailing Our Way to More Fulfilling Personal Lives," *(Newark, NJ) Star-Ledger*, January 10, 2010.

Source Notes

Introduction: Online Victimization

1. Quoted in Angela Monroe, "Police Search Computer of Suspected Online Predator," KMIR-TV, September 29, 2011. www.kmir6.com.

2. Quoted in Pete Williams, "MySpace, Facebook Attract Online Predators," NBC News, February 3, 2006. www.msnbc.msn.com.

3. US Department of State, "Internet Dating and Romance Scams." http://travel.state.gov.

4. Quoted in redOrbit, "Rising Number of Sexual Predators Overwhelming," March 21, 2009. www.redorbit.com.

5. Janis Wolak, David, Finkelhor, and Kimberly Mitchell, "Trends in Arrests of 'Online Predators,'" University of New Hampshire Crimes Against Children Research Center. www.unh.edu.

6. Larry Magid, "Online Predation an Exaggerated Problem," CBS News, February 11, 2009. www.cbsnews.com.

7. Mothers Against Drunk Driving, "Statistics." www.madd.org.

8. Donna Rice Hughes, "Sexual Predators Online," ProtectKids. www.protectkids.com.

9. Jason Behr, "Are Dangers of Cyberbullying and Online Exploitation for Children and Teenagers Exaggerated?," www.maxupdates.tv.

Chapter One: What Are the Origins of the Online Predator Problem?

10. J. Suler, "The Online Disinhibition Effect," http://users.rider.edu/~suler/psycyber/disinhibit.html.

11. J. Suler, "The Online Disinhibition Effect."

12. Frederick S. Lane, *Cybertraps for the Young*. Chicago: NTI Up-stream, 2011, p. 20.

13. Lane, *Cybertraps for the Young*, p 12.

14. David Jacobson, "Impression Formation in Cyberspace: Online Expectations and Offline Experiences in Text-Based Virtual Communities," http://jcmc.indiana.edu/vol5/issue1/jacobson.html.

15. Diane Carbo, "Healing Loneliness: The Trap of the Internet Romance Con," http://ezinearticles.com/?Healing-Loneliness: -The-Trap-of-the-Internet-Romance-Con&id=5493205.

16. Diane Carbo, "Healing Loneliness."

17. Richard Guerry, *Public and Permanent: The Golden Rule of the 21st Century*. Bloomington, IN: Balboa, 2011, p. 22

18. Guerry, *Public and Permanent*, p. 21.

19. Wolak, Finkelhor, and Mitchell, "Trends in Arrests of 'Online Predators,'" p. 1.

20. Janis Wolak, David Finkelhor, Kimberly J. Mitchell, and Michele L. Ybarra, "Online 'Predators' and Their Victims: Myths, Realities, and Implications for Prevention and Treatment," *American Psychologist*, February/March 2008, p. 112. www.apa.org.

21. InternetSafetyRules.net, "Why and How of the Importance of Internet Safety Rules," May 19, 2010. http://internetsafetyrules.net.

Chapter Two: Who Is Most at Risk from Online Predators?

22. Michael Ryan, "How Internet Predators Select Their Victims," Safer Internet. www.safer-internet.net.

23. Ryan, "How Internet Predators Select Their Victims."

24. University of New Hampshire Media Relations, "'Internet Predator' Stereotypes Debunked in New Study," press release, February 18, 2008. www.unh.edu.

25. Quoted in Lane, *Cybertraps for the Young*, pp. 31–32.

26. Quoted in Salynn Boyles, "Teens Are Hardwired for Risky Behavior," Web MD. www.webmd.com.

27. Quoted in Boyles, "Teens Are Hardwired for Risky Behavior."

28. Quoted in Boyles, "Teens Are Hardwired for Risky Behavior."

29. Larry Magid, "Online Predation an Exaggerated Problem."

30. Federal Bureau of Investigation, "Fraud Target: Senior Citizens." www.fbi.gov.

31. Quoted in Melissa Singer, "Billions Lost as Online Criminals Target Young," *Sydney Morning Herald* (Australia), September 20, 2010. www.smh.com.au.

32. Quoted in Kimberly Palmer, "MTV's 'Teen Mom': Victim of Financial Fraud," Money, *US News*, September 8, 2010. http://money.usnews.com.

33. Quoted in Bob Sullivan, "Seduced into Scams: Online Lovers Often Duped," MSNBC. www.msnbc.msn.com.

34. Quoted in Sullivan, "Seduced into Scams."

35. Quoted in Sullivan, "Seduced into Scams."

Chapter Three: Are Internet Dangers Exaggerated?

36. Lisa H. Warren, "Stranger Danger—More Real than Some Want to Believe," HubPages. http://lisahwarren.hubpages.com.

37. Quoted in Larry Magid. "Net Safety Task Force Says Predation Risk Exaggerated," Safe Kids. www.safekids.com.

38. Wolak, Finkelhor, Mitchell, and Ybarra, "Online 'Predators' and Their Victims," p. 113.

39. Benjamin Radford, "Predator Panic: A Closer Look," Committee for Skeptical Inquiry. www.csicop.org.

40. Radford, "Predator Panic: A Closer Look."

41. Quoted in Benjamin Radford, "Predator Panic: Reality Check on Sex Offenders," Live Science, May 16, 2006. www.live science.com.

42. Radford, "Predator Panic: Reality Check on Sex Offenders."

43. Mike Thomas, "Reports of Mayhem, Fear Distort Reality: Crime on the Decline," *Orlando Sentinel*, May 11, 2011. www.orlandosentinel.com.

44. Thomas, "Reports of Mayhem, Fear Distort Reality."

45. Quoted in Thomas, "Reports of Mayhem, Fear Distort Reality."

46. Child Welfare Research Institute, "Making the Web Safe for Kids." http://childwelfare.com.

47. International Mass-Marketing Fraud Working Group, "Mass-Marketing Fraud: A Threat Assessment," US Immigration and Customs Enforcement, June 2010, p. 9. www.ice.gov.

48. International Mass-Marketing Fraud Working Group, "Mass-Marketing Fraud," p. 3.

49. Kostas Mavropalias, "Cybercrime & Cyberterrorism: Inducing Anxiety and Fear on Individuals," (blog), February 23, 2011. http://iconof.com.

Chapter Four: Can the Legal System Stop Online Predators?

50. Quoted in Chris Perry, "Prosecutors Want to Try Teen as Adult in Craigslist Job Ad Killings," CNN, January 24, 2012. http://articles.cnn.com.

51. Kate Connolly, "Paedophile Trap TV Show Backfires on Presenter," *Guardian* [Manchester, UK], October 19, 2010. www.guardian.co.uk.

52. Thomas A. Pavlinic, Premier Defense Group. www.premierdefensegroup.com.

53. Quoted in Mark Bowden, "A Crime of Shadows," Culture, *Vanity Fair*, December 2009. www.vanityfair.com.

54. Bowden, "A Crime of Shadows."

55. Ted Belling, "Online Predator Sexual Stings," Case Law 4 Cops. www.caselaw4cops.net.

56. International Mass-Marketing Fraud Working Group, "Mass-Marketing Fraud," p. 19.

Chapter Five: Can Prevention Efforts Protect Online Users from Predators?

57. Quoted in Michael Miller, "Parents of Teens Confront Web Safety," *Daily Pilot* (Orange County, CA), February 24, 2006. http://dailypilot.com.

58. Quoted in Miller, "Parents of Teens Confront Web Safety."

59. Quoted in Winston-Salem/Forsyth County School System Instructional Technology Division, "Online Safety Report Discourages Scare Tactics," In Touch, June 14, 2010. http://wsfcsintouch.blogspot.com.

60. Denise Witmer, "3 Reasons Why Parents Shouldn't Use Scare Tactics," About.com Teens. http://parentingteens.about.com.

61. Lane, *Cybertraps for the Young*, p. 44.

62. Quoted in Online Mom, "Teens Still Exercising Poor Judgment Online," July 2010. www.theonlinemom.com.

63. Quoted in Miller, "Parents of Teens Confront Web Safety."

64. Lane, *Cybertraps for the Young*, pp. 60–61.

65. Miller, "Parents of Teens Confront Web Safety."

66. Wolak, Finkelhor, and Mitchell, "Trends in Arrests of 'Online Predators,'" p. 8.

67. Wolak, Finkelhor, and Mitchell, "Trends in Arrests of 'Online Predators,'" p. 8.

68. Family Online Safety Institute, State of Online Safety Report, p. 56. www.fosi.org.

69. Family Online Safety Institute, "State of Online Safety Report," p. 56.

70. Quoted in Saabira Chaudhuri, "Criminalizing False Identities: The End of Online Anonymity?," Fast Company, December 2, 2008. www.fastcompany.com.

71. Electronic Privacy Information Center, "Internet Anonymity." http://epic.org.

72. Nancy Willard, "Techno-Panic & 21st Century Education," Center for Safe and Responsible Internet Use, p. 4. www.csriu .org.

73. Steve Rendall, "The Online Predator Panic," FAIR. www.fair. org.

74. Quoted in *Daily Mail* [London, UK], "A Third of Internet Users Too Scared of Fraud to Hand Over Credit Card Details for Online Shopping," May 11, 2009. www.dailymail.co.uk.

75. Willard, "Techno-Panic & 21st Century Education," p. 4.

Index

Note: Boldface page numbers indicate illustrations.

Acosta, Jim, 45
American Association of Retired Persons (AARP), 31, 32
American Civil Liberties Union (ACLU), 54
American Psychological Association, 26

Beasley, Richard, 52
Belling, Ted, 60
Bowden, Mark, 58–59
brain
    regions of, **29**
    teenage, is immature, 29–30
    teenage, risk taking and, 29–30
Burdynski, George Stanley, 19–20

Carbo, Diane, 15–16
Chandler, Rebecca, 30–31
chat rooms, 12
    false identities on, 7–8
    misimpressions formed in, 14–15
    percentage of youth using, 40
    safety tips for, 68
    teens soliciting sexual conversations in, 28
child pornography, 20
    operation focusing on, 63
children/adolescents
    demonstrating vulnerability of, 64–67
    risk taking by, 29–30
    sexual curiosity of, 28
    sharing information online, prevalence of, 69, 77
    surveys on Internet activities among, 40–41

See also teenagers
Child Welfare Research Institute, 46
Children's Internet Protection Act (CIPA, 2000), 70
computer forensics, 63
Condrat, Louis, 56
Craigslist killers, 52–53
Crimes Against Children Research Center (University of New Hampshire), 9, 19, 43, 67
    on misperceptions about online predators, 22
    on prevalence of deception by online predators, 41–42
    on susceptibility of boys to online sex crimes, 28
    on use of term "predator," 20–21
cyberstalking, 32
CyberTipline (National Center for Missing and Exploited Children), 50
Cybertraps for the Young (Lane), 14, 28

Data Privacy Day, 11
Dateline NBC (TV program)
    To Catch a Predator (TV series), 55–57
dating scams, 35–37
DatingSitesReviews.com (website), 7
Davis, Scott, 52–53
Department of Justice, US, 25, 54
Department of State, US, 7
DeWine, Mike, 53
digital certificates, 51
Digital Youth Project, 10
disinhibition effect, 12–13

Electronic Privacy Information
    Center, 74
entrapment, 56–57

Facebook, 6, 76
    creation of fake pages on, 32, 60
    demonstrating students' vulner-
        abilities on, 64–65
    number of active users of, 8
    use in North America *vs.* in Asia,
        11
false identities
    lack of punishment for perpetra-
        tors of, 61–62
    prevalence on dating websites, 7
    See also chat rooms; online
        predators
Family Online Safety Institute, 11
Federal Bureau of Investigation
    (FBI), 20, 31, 33
Felix, Jesus, 60–61
Ferguson, Julie, 35
filtering software, 70–71
financial predation/predators, 14
    advance fee frauds by, 33, 34–35
        in Nigeria, prevalence of, 34
    challenges presented by, 62
    dangers of, 47–48
    dating scams used by, 35, 36–37
    seniors as targets of, 31–33
    wire money transfers and, 58
    young adults as targets of, 33–35

Geiger, Ralph, 53
Giedd, Jay, 30
Girl Scout Research Institute, 25
Google Earth (website), 65, **66**
Graham, Michael, 69
Gregory, Mark, 33
grooming, 26–27
Guerry, Richard, 18–19

Hansen, Chris, 55
Henderson, Les, 16
Hore, Cameron Stuart, 26
Hughes, Donna Rice, 9, 10

identity theft insurance, 50
information. *See* personal

information
Institute of Criminality (Australia),
    14
International Mass-Marketing
    Fraud Working Group (IMMF-
    WG), 46–48, 62
Internet
    beginnings of, 17–18
    idea of community redefined by,
        18–19
    malicious impersonation on,
        61–62
    number of subscribers globally, 8
    restricting sex offenders' access
        to, 54
    transfer of money over, 33
Internet Crimes Against Children
    task force, 57
Internet Safety Technical Task
    Force, 42, 43
InternetSafetyRules.net (website),
    22–23

Jacobson, David, 14–15
Journal of Adolescent Health, 40
judgment, impact of sleep depriva-
    tion on, 21

Kowalski, James A., Jr., 20

Lane, Frederick S., 13, 14, 28,
    68–69
Larrabee, Raven, 31
Laur, Darren, 64–65
Leak, Steven (Bruce), 20
Leutheusser-Schnarrenberger,
    Sabine, 57
Lynch, Joseph, 20

Magid, Larry, 10, 30, 43
malware, Internet fraud involving,
    63
McAfee, Inc., 38, 40, 69, 77
media
    crime complex and, 49
    distort prevalence of child preda-
        tion, 45–46
    promote distorted view of online
        predators, 43

role in public education, 49–50
Media Awareness Network, 38
Miller, Michael, 70
minor, legal definitions of, 43–44
missing children, majority of cases
 not associated with sex offenders, 45
money
 transfers over Internet, 33
 wire transfers via Western Union,
  58
Mooney, Tracy, 69, 76
Mothers Against Drunk Driving
 (MADD), 10
MySpace, 7, 61, 65, 76

National Center for Missing and
 Exploited Children, 50, 63, 77
National Cyber Security Alliance,
 77
National Institute of Mental Health
 (NIMH), 30
Nigerian Advance Fee Scam (4-1-9
 fraud), 34
Norton Online Family Report, 77

Online predation/predators, **33**
 caution used by, 15
 false identities used by, 7–9
 misperceptions of, 21, 22, 43
 profiles of, 20–21,
 risk assessment of, 9–10
 scope of problems caused by, 9
 social networking sites and, 6–7,
  22–23
 See also financial predation/preda-
  tors; sexual predation/predators
Online Safety and Technology
 Working Group (OSTWG), 67
Operation Save Our Children, 63
opinion polls. *See* surveys

parents
 importance of rule-setting by,
  22–23
 monitoring of teens' online
  activities by, 69–70
 percentage of teen girls informing
  of online sexual solicitation/

bullying, 25
 prevalence of teens' hiding Internet activities from, 40–41
Pauley, David, 53
Pavlinic, Thomas A., 55, 57–58
personal information
 of friends, dangers of revealing,
  47
 permanence of, once online, 18,
  72
 phishing for, 38
 sharing of, 7, 68–69
  age and likelihood of, 14
  dangers of, 23
  demonstrating to students
   dangers of, 64–69
  prevalence among teens, 69, 77
 transfer of money over sites not
  protecting, 33
Perverted-Justice. *See* Dateline NBC
phishing, 38
physical violence, percentage of
 sexual exploitation involving, 50
polls. *See* surveys
predators/predation. *See* financial
 predation/predators; online
 predators/predation; sexual
 predators/predation
Price, Jennifer, 9
Protecting Children in the 21st
 Century Act (2008), 71
The Psychology of Cyberspace (Suler),
 12–13

Radford, Benjamin, 44–45
Rafferty, Brogan, 52, **56**
Rochester Institute for Technology,
 40
Ryan, Michael, 27

Sackman, Jeffrey Thomas, 6
seniors, as targets of financial predators, 31–33
sexual predation/predators
 age of, 42–43
 increase in, correlates to increased
  Internet use, 51
 against minors, online crime as
  percentage of arrests for, 11

numbers registered *vs.* accounted for, in US, 63

percentage involving physical violence, 50

profile of, 20–22

restricting Internet access by, 54

sting operations targeting, 54–55, 63

  pitfalls/advantages of, 59–60

susceptibility of boys to, 28

use of deception by, prevalence of, 41–42

use of photos to determine age/gender of victims, 15

Singer, Melissa, 33

sleep deprivation, 21

Smalley, Theresa, 36–37

social networking sites

  access of private information by employees of, 72

  demonstrating students' vulnerability on, 64–69

  popularity of, 23–24

  See also Facebook; MySpace

spam, 38

Stanford, Suzanne, 65

Steinberg, Laurence, 29–30

Suler, John, 12–13

surveys

  of business, on cyber security, 77

  of teenage girls telling parents about online sexual solicitation/bullying, 25

  on trust in online advice/recommendations, 14

teenagers

  average time spent online per week, 25

  brain of, **29**

risk taking and, 29–30, 73

education of, about online predators, 71–72

parental monitoring of online activities, 68–70

risk of online predation and, 72, 73

scare tactics do not change online behaviors of, 67, 68–69

television, undercover antipredator efforts on, 55–57

Thomas, Mike, 44, 45

To Catch a Predator (TV program), 55–56

Trust (film), 41

University of New Hampshire. *See* Crimes Against Children Research Center

Vanity Fair (magazine), 58

victimization, online, risk for, 9–10

victims

  grooming of, by online predators, 26–27

  profile of, 24

  underreporting of experiences by, 40–42

video chats, 77

Violet, Robert, 19, 20

Warren, Lisa H., 39

Western Union, 58

Williams, Pete, 7

Witmer, Denise, 68, 69

World Wide Web, 18

Yarrow, Kit, 35

Ybarra, Michele L., 22

Picture Credits

Cover: iStockphoto.com

Maury Aaseng: 29

AP Images: 56, 61, 66, 75

© David Brabyn/Corbis: 49

© Macduff Everton/Corbis: 17

Landov Media: 23, 36

Thinkstock/Creatas: 8

Thinkstock/iStockphoto.com: 42

About the Author

Patricia D. Netzley has written dozens of books for children, teens, and adults. She has also worked as an editor and a writing instructor. She is a member of the Society of Children's Book Writers and Illustrators (SCBWI) and the Romance Writers of America (RWA).